The Flowers at a Glance

Pictorial Guide in Alphabetical Order, by Common Name

Ajuga
p. 68

Anemone
p. 72

Artemisia
p. 76

Aster
p. 80

Astilbe
p. 84

Bellflower
p. 92

Basket-of-Gold
p. 88

Bergamot
p. 96

Bergenia
p. 100

Black-Eyed Susan
p. 104

Bleeding Heart
p. 110

Boltonia
p. 114

Blazing Star
p. 108

Blanket Flower
p. 106

Brunnera
p. 116

Butterfly Weed
p. 118

Candytuft
p. 120

Cardinal Flower
p. 122

Catmint
p. 126

Clematis
p. 134

Chrysanthemum
p. 130

Columbine
p. 138

Coral Bells
p. 142

Coreopsis
p. 146

Cornflower
p. 150

Crocosmia
p. 152

Daylily
p. 154

Dead Nettle
p. 158

Euphorbia
p. 166

False Indigo
p. 170

Delphinium
p. 162

False Sunflower
p. 172

Foamflower
p. 174

Foxglove
p. 176

Geum
p. 180

Golden Marguerite
p. 188

Hardy Geranium
p. 190

Globe Thistle
p. 182

Goat's Beard
p. 184

Hens and Chicks
p. 194

Hosta
p. 200

Iris
p. 204

Hollyhock
p. 196

Joe-Pye Weed
p. 208

Lady's Mantle
p. 210

Lamb's Ears
p. 214

Ligularia
p. 220

Lychnis
p. 228

Lavender
p. 216

Lungwort
p. 224

Mallow
p. 230

Meadow Rue
p. 234

Meadowsweet
p. 238

Monkshood
p. 242

Obedient Plant
p. 246

Oriental Poppy
p. 248

Penstemon
p. 250

Peony
p. 254

Phlox
p. 258

Pincushion Flower
p. 262

Pinks
p. 264

Plume Poppy
p. 268

Primrose
p. 270

Purple Coneflower
p. 274

Red-Hot Poker
p. 276

Rockcress
p. 278

Rodgersia
p. 280

Rose Mallow
p. 282

Russian Sage
p. 284

Sea Holly
p. 286

Sneezeweed
p. 296

Sedum
p. 290

Shasta Daisy
p. 294

Soapwort
p. 298

Speedwell
p. 300

Spiderwort
p. 304

Stokes' Aster
p. 306

Sundrops
p. 308

Thrift
p. 310

Thyme
p. 312

Vinca
p. 318

Yarrow
p. 322

Trillium
p. 316

Wild Ginger
p. 320

Introduction

IT'S BEEN ALMOST TWO DECADES since perennial plants began their ascension to stardom in Michigan gardens, and in the past few years the rise has been meteoric. Michigan gardeners wanted to do more than just expand the diversity of plants in their gardens. Some grew tired of using the same old annuals year after year; others yearned for more color, more texture, more fragrance—an ever-changing palette that would span the seasons with panache. And these plant-hungry gardeners wanted plants that were cold hardy, plants that would live through winter and rise again in spring to put on another fabulous show.

Perennials are generally described as herbaceous, or non-woody, plants that live for three years or more. Most die back over the summer or in fall, send up new shoots in spring and live for many years. Their longevity varies from short-lived perennials such as Hollyhock, which may live only a year or two (but which is considered to be perennial because of its profuse offsetting and re-seeding) to long-lived perennials, such as peonies, which have been known to thrive for more than a century. Most perennials die back to the ground when they go dormant, but some, such as coral bells and pinks, are evergreen and retain their foliage throughout the winter.

Others, including thymes, Lavender and Russian Sage, are called sub-shrubs, because they have somewhat woody branches.

The temperate climate of Michigan, with its warm summers, cold winters and reasonably dependable rainfall, is ideal for growing a wide range of perennials. Gardeners across the state experience many of the same climatic features, but temperature and soil conditions do vary and almost every garden has its own unique characteristics. The key is to plant the right perennial in the right place. No matter how challenging the site, some perennials will always flourish and supply an impressive array of colors, sizes and forms.

This versatility, and the beauty and permanence of perennials, explains their ever-growing popularity.

The growing season is longer in the south of Michigan than the north but is long enough all over for many perennials to thrive. As well, winter is cold enough across the state to provide the dormancy required by many perennials, such as peonies, to set flowers for the following summer. The lakes can have a tempering influence on winter weather, giving the entire state warmer temperatures than other places at the same latitude, with the warmest temperatures along the east shore of Lake Michigan.

Although winter is cold across the state, the degree of snow cover varies. Snow cover is important because it provides excellent insulation for dormant perennials, maintaining consistent soil temperatures and providing shelter from drying winds. Gardens near the lakes receive more snow than gardens farther inland. As well, northern gardeners are at an advantage because the consistently lower temperatures maintain the snow cover most winters. Southern gardens are susceptible to freeze–thaw cycles and less consistent snow cover, killing some plants that might survive in a better insulated but colder garden. A thick layer of organic mulch will provide protection in gardens where a snow cover is undependable.

Spring is generally cool and moist. The last frost occurs between late April and late May, depending on where you are in Michigan. Spring weather is also affected by the lakes. Close to the lakes, the cool, wet spring weather may be drawn out, delaying planting and encouraging

rot in perennials that dislike such conditions. Farther inland the last frost may occur later, but warmer, drier weather may arrive at the same time or even sooner than it does for those gardens closer to the lakes.

Summer tends to be hot and humid. Excessively hot days that may harm plants can occur all over the state but are more common and frequent in the south. Places with fewer hot days actually allow an expanded selection of perennials, because many plants thrive in more moderate climates. Rain is generally consistent and regular enough across Michigan to keep supplemental watering to a minimum for all but the most moisture loving of perennials. Both excessive rain and excessive drought can occur in summer, but vigilant gardeners can usually help their gardens through such summers without the loss of many plants. Good garden preparation will encourage a balance between moisture retention and drainage.

Fall is possibly the most ideal month for gardening in Michigan. Days are warm and nights cool, providing ideal conditions for many perennials. Though the first frost can happen in September, many perennials will continue to bloom up until the first hard frost. Gardens in southern Michigan may not see frost until well into October.

The United States Department of Agriculture (USDA) hardiness zone map (the basis for the map on p. 15) is the standard that both growers and gardeners use to help determine if a plant can survive cold temperatures. This system was developed for

woody plants because they remain exposed during the winter, but it is a useful tool for perennial gardeners too. Most of Michigan is designated as Zone 5, meaning that the average low winter temperatures range between –10° and –20° F. However, a few areas in the Lower Peninsula benefit from the moderating effect of the Great Lakes and are designated as Zone 6, with average lows between 0° and –10° F. Conversely, the Upper Peninsula and north-central parts of the Lower Peninsula have colder pockets designated a frigid Zone 3, where winter temperatures may dip as low as –40° F.

But the adventurous gardener soon discovers that although this zone hardiness designation is an

important consideration when purchasing plants, it is only a guideline. Many factors, such as snow cover and soil moisture, contribute to successful overwintering of perennials. For example, a given perennial may be hardy in Zone 6 because of the warm winter temperatures, and in Zone 3 in areas of consistent snow cover, but it may not survive in Zone 5 if the snow mostly melts away between falls, leaving the ground exposed. As well, almost every garden has favorable microclimates: pockets that are protected from the elements, and spaces where the soil remains warmer in winter than in the rest of the garden. These pockets may be havens for plants that would not be considered cold hardy elsewhere in your garden. Influences on microclimate include proximity to buildings, soil drainage qualities and topographic features such as low, cold hollows and windswept hilltops.

The challenge of gardening with plants that are borderline hardy— those everyone says can't possibly grow here—is part of the fun of growing perennials, so don't let hardiness guidelines limit your experimentation. Unlike trees and shrubs, perennials are relatively inexpensive and easy to share with friends and neighbors, so the more varieties you try, the more likely you'll be to discover plants that love to grow in your own garden. When it comes to perennials, the best advice is to dig in and 'just grow for it.'

One of the greatest assets of gardening in Michigan is the creativity and enthusiasm of the many people involved. From one end of the state to the other, you will find individuals, growers, breeders, societies, schools, publications and public gardens all devoted to the advancement and enjoyment of gardening in Michigan. You will have no trouble

finding information, encourage-
ment and fruitful debate; Michigan
gardeners embody a knowledge of
planting and propagation methods,
a precision in identifying specific
plants and a plethora of passionate
opinions on what is best for any
little patch of ground.

Garden clubs and plant societies
are great resources. There are chap-
ters of the Federated Garden Clubs
of Michigan (989-682-9125) and
National Women's Farm and Garden
Club in cities throughout Michigan.
Check the gardening calendars in
local papers and the *Michigan
Gardener* magazine (248-594-5563)
for meeting times and places.

Many public gardens offer educa-
tional programs along with volun-
teer opportunities to help advance
the art and science of gardening.
The Master Gardener Program of
Michigan State University Extension
has trained thousands of Michigan
residents as Master Gardeners. For
information on the Master Gardener Program in your county, call
the State Master Gardener Coordi-
nator at 517-353-3774 or visit the
following website:
<http://www.msue.msu.edu/
mastergardener/>. For a list of public
gardens and other horticultural centers in Michigan, see p. 331.

Hardiness Zones Map

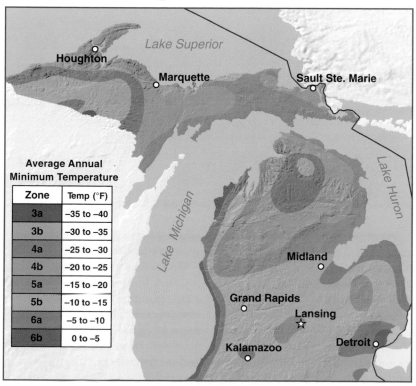

Perennial Gardens

PERENNIALS CAN BE USED ALONE or combined with other plants. They establish a bridge between the permanent structure provided by trees and shrubs, often referred to as the bones of the garden, and the temporary color provided by annuals. Perennials can be included in any garden, regardless of its size or style. From the riot of color in a cottage garden to the cool, soothing shades of green in a woodland garden, and from an expansive, impressive bed to a welcoming cluster of pots on a front doorstep, perennials open up a world of design possibilities for even the most inexperienced gardener.

When planning your garden it is important to decide what you like. If you are enamored with the plants in your garden, you are more likely to take proper care of them. Decide on what style of garden you like as well as what plants you like. Think about the gardens you have most admired in your neighborhood, in books or while visiting friends. Use these ideas as starting points for planning your own garden.

Decide how much time you have to devote to your garden. With just a little planning and preparation you can create an easy-care garden. Begin by choosing plants that perform well, require little maintenance and are generally not plagued by any pest and diseases. They will help you to create a low-maintenance garden that will give you time to relax and enjoy the fruits of your labor.

Try to select perennials that flower at different times in order to have some part of your garden flowering all season. The Quick Reference Chart on p. 332 will help you.

As well, consider the size and shape of the perennials you choose. Pick a variety of forms to make your garden more interesting. The size of your garden influences these decisions, but do not limit a small garden to small perennials or a large garden to large perennials. Use a balanced combination of plant sizes that are in scale with their specific location. (See Quick Reference Chart, p. 332.)

Perennials present limitless choices in color. Not only do flower colors vary, but foliage colors vary as well, from yellow, gray, blue or purple to any multitude of greens. Different colors have different effects on our senses. Cool colors like blue, purple and green are soothing; they seem to recede, making small spaces appear bigger. The warm colors like red, orange and yellow advance, appearing to fill large spaces while adding excitement. (See Quick Reference Chart, p. 332.)

Texture can also create a sense of space. Larger leaves are considered coarse in texture, and when viewed from a distance they make spaces seem smaller and more shaded. Small leaves, or those that are finely divided, are considered fine in texture and create a sense of greater space and light. Foliage can be bold or flimsy, coarse or refined; it can be big or small, light or dark; it can be one solid color or patterned with stripes, splashes, dots and blobs. The leaf surfaces may be shiny, fuzzy, silky, rough or smooth. Whole gardens can be designed solely on the basis of texture.

Foliage can provide year-round interest in every garden. Remember that a good perennial garden is about more than just flowers; the stems and leaves of the plants make up an integral part of the design. The famous white gardens at Sissinghurst, England, were designed, not to showcase a haphazard collection of white flowers, but to remove the distraction of color and allow the eye to linger on the foliage, to appreciate its subtle appeal. Flowers come and go, but a garden planned with careful attention to foliage will always be interesting.

Coarse-textured Perennials
Bergenia
Black-eyed Susan
Daylily
Hollyhock
Hosta
Lungwort
Purple Coneflower
Rose Mallow
Sedum 'Autumn Joy'

Hosta

Fine-textured Perennials
Artemisia
Astilbe
Bleeding Heart
Columbine
Coreopsis
Lady's Mantle
Meadow Rue
Thyme

Astilbe

Low-maintenance Perennials
Ajuga*
Aster
Black-eyed Susan
Butterfly Weed
Catmint
Coral Bells
Daylily
Dead Nettle*
Hardy Geranium
Hosta
Lady's Mantle
Pinks
Purple Coneflower
Russian Sage
Sedum 'Autumn Joy'
Yarrow*
(*may become invasive)

Coral Bells

Getting Started

ONCE YOU HAVE SOME IDEAS about what you want in your garden, consider the growing conditions. Plants grown in conditions that match their needs are healthier and less prone to pest and disease problems than plants growing in stressful conditions. Some plants considered high maintenance become low maintenance when grown in the right conditions.

Do not attempt to make your garden match the growing conditions of the plants you like. Instead, choose plants to match your garden conditions. The levels of light, the type of soil and the amount of exposure in your garden provide guidelines that make plant selection easier. A sketch of your garden, drawn on graph paper, may help you organize the various considerations you want to keep in mind as you plan. Mark on the map areas that are shaded, wet, windy and so on. Becoming familiar with your growing conditions can prevent costly mistakes—plan ahead rather than correct later.

Light

Buildings, trees, fences and the time of day influence the amount of light that gets into your garden. There are four basic categories of light in the garden: full sun, partial shade, light shade and full shade. Knowing what light is available in different areas helps in deciding where to put each plant.

Full sun locations receive direct sunlight all or most of the day, as would, for example, a south-facing wall. **Partial shade** or partial sun locations receive direct sun for part of the day and shade for the rest. An east- or west-facing wall gets only partial sun. **Light shade** locations receive shade most or all of the day, but some sun penetrates through to ground level. The ground underneath a small-leaved tree is often lightly shaded, with dapples of sun visible on the ground beneath the tree. **Full shade** locations receive no direct sunlight. The north side of a house is considered to be in full shade.

It is important to remember that the intensity of sun or shade can vary. For example, heat can become trapped and magnified between buildings in a city, baking all but the most heat-tolerant plants in a concrete oven. Conversely, the sheltered hollow in the shade that protects your heat-hating plants in the humid summer heat may become a frost trap in winter, killing tender plants that should otherwise survive. In both cases, good organic mulch on the soil will help temper these extreme effects.

Full sun garden

Perennials for Full Sun
Artemisia
Aster
Basket-of-gold
Coreopsis
Daylily
Mallow
Phlox
Russian Sage
Sedum
Thyme
Yarrow

Perennials for Full Shade
Ajuga
Astilbe
Bleeding Heart
Brunnera
Dead Nettle
Hosta
Lungwort
Monkshood
Primrose
Sweet Woodruff
Vinca
Wild Ginger

Sun-loving Russian Sage (above),
shady border (below)

Soil

Matching plants with the soil conditions they prefer lays the foundation for a thriving garden. Healthy garden soil holds air, water, nutrients and organic matter, elements that are necessary for many plant functions. Roots also use soil as an anchor to hold the plant body upright.

Soil is made up of particles of different sizes. Sand particles are the largest. Water drains quickly out of sandy soil, and nutrients are quickly washed away. Sand has lots of air space and doesn't compact easily. Clay particles are the smallest and can only be seen through a microscope. Water penetrates and drains very slowly through clay soil. Clay holds the most nutrients, but there is very little room for air, and clay compacts quite easily. Most soil is made up of a combination of different particle sizes. These soils are called loams.

Particle size is one influence on the drainage and moisture-holding properties of your soil; slope is another. Rocky soil on a hillside will probably drain very quickly and should be reserved for those plants that prefer a very well drained soil.

Low-lying areas tend to retain water longer, and some areas may rarely drain at all. Moist areas suit plants that require a consistent water supply, and areas that stay wet can be used for plants that prefer boggy conditions.

Most soils in Michigan were deposited by receding glaciers and can vary greatly. They may be rich and easy to work, or they may be of poorer quality, consisting mainly of sand, clay or rock. Poor-quality soil, whether it be clay or sand, can be improved by adding organic matter, such as sphagnum peat moss, shredded leaves, compost or composted manure. Drainage can be improved in very wet areas by adding a combination of organic matter and gravel or sharp sand to the soil, or by building raised beds. Keep in mind that adding sand or gravel to heavy clay without organic matter makes cement.

Some perennials thrive in difficult soils and may be useful to you, because amending soils can be a long process.

Perennials for Sandy Soil
Artemisia
Basket-of-gold
Cornflower
Euphorbia
Rose Campion
Russian Sage
Thyme

Perennials for Clay Soil
Ajuga
Black-eyed Susan
Blazing Star
Foamflower
Goldenrod
Hardy Geranium
Hosta
New England Aster
Purple Coneflower
Vinca

New England Aster

Rose Campion & Phlox

Another important aspect of soil to consider is the pH. This is the scale on which the acidity or alkalinity of soil is measured. A pH of 7 is neutral; higher numbers indicate an alkaline soil and lower numbers an acidic soil. The pH of the soil determines a plant's ability to take up nutrients. Although some plants prefer acid or alkaline soils, most grow best in a neutral pH of 6.5 to 7. Soils in Michigan can vary from alkaline to acidic, but alkaline soils tend to prevail.

Before amending your soil, have it tested. Your County Cooperative Extension Service will provide a soil profile that indicates the proper amendments needed to improve the soil in your garden. Acidic soil can be made more alkaline by adding horticultural lime, while alkaline soil can be made more acidic by adding sulfur or iron sulfate. Note, though, that altering the pH of your soil takes a long time, often many years, and is not easy. If you are trying to grow only one or two plants that require soil of a different pH than that in your garden, consider growing them in a container or raised bed, where it will be easier to control and amend the pH as needed.

Perennials for Moist Soil

Astilbe
Bleeding Heart
Cardinal Flower
Goat's Beard
Hosta
Iris
Lady's Mantle
Ligularia
Lungwort
Meadowsweet
Monkshood
Primrose
Rose Mallow

Perennials for Dry Soil

Artemisia
Basket-of-gold
Butterfly Weed
Coreopsis
Lamb's Ears
Pinks
Russian Sage
Sedum
Sundrops
Thrift
Yarrow

Lamb's Ears & Thyme

Primrose

Exposure

Finally, consider the exposure in your garden. Wind, heat, cold and rain are some of the elements to which your garden is exposed, and plants tolerate to varying degrees the damage these forces can cause. Buildings, walls, fences, hills, hedges and trees can all influence your garden's exposure.

Wind in particular can cause extensive damage to your plants. Plants can become dehydrated in windy locations because they may not be able to draw water out of the soil fast enough to replace the water that is lost through the leaves. Tall, stiff-stemmed perennials can be knocked over or broken by strong winds. Some plants that do not require staking in a sheltered location may need to be staked in a more exposed one. Use plants that are recommended for exposed locations, or buffer the effect of the wind with a hedge or trees. A solid wall creates turbulence on the leeward side, while a looser structure, such as a hedge, breaks up the force of the wind and protects a larger area.

Perennials for Exposed Locations
Basket-of-gold
Candytuft
Columbine
Creeping Phlox
Euphorbia
Penstemon
Sedum (groundcover species)
Thyme

Penstemon

Preparing the Garden

TAKING THE TIME TO PROPERLY PREPARE your flowerbeds will save you time and effort later in the growing season. Thoroughly digging over your beds, removing all weeds and amending the soil with organic matter before planting are the first steps in caring for your perennials.

Turning compost into beds

Removing weeds & debris

Organic Soil Amendments

All soils, from the heaviest clay to the lightest sand, benefit from the addition of organic matter. Some of the best organic additives include chopped leaves, compost, very well rotted manure and composted bark because they add nutrients as well as improving the structure of the soil. These additives improve heavy clay soils by loosening them and allowing air and water to penetrate. Organic matter improves sandy or light soils by increasing their ability to retain water and nutrients.

Organic matter is introduced to the garden in two ways. For empty beds, mix organic matter into the soil with a garden fork in spring, when your soil is ready to work. For an established garden, add a 2–3" layer of organic mulch to the soil surface and leave it there for the entire season. Earthworms will pull pieces of that mulch down into the soil for lunch. Within a few months, worms and other decomposers will break down the organic matter, releasing nutrients for plants, and as a bonus, their activities will help aerate the soil.

Compost worms

Wooden compost bins (above)

Plastic compost bins (center),
material for compost (below)

Composting

In forests, meadows and other natural environments, organic debris, such as leaves and other plant bits, breaks down on the soil surface and the nutrients are gradually made available to the plants that are growing there. We can emulate that same process in our own backyard with a compost pile. Compost is a great additive for your perennial garden, and good composting methods help reduce pest and disease problems.

Compost can be made in a pile, in a wooden box or in a purchased compost bin. Two methods can be used; neither is complicated, but one requires more effort.

The 'active' or hot composting method requires you to turn the pile every week or so during the growing season. Frequent turning creates compost faster, but because the compost generates a lot of heat, some beneficial microorganisms that help fight diseases are killed. If you prefer the active approach to composting, several good books are available that give step-by-step details of the process.

For most gardeners, the easier method, 'passive' or cold composting, is the more practical approach. Making a passive compost pile involves simply dumping most yard waste into a pile. This organic stuff may include small plants thinned from the vegetable garden, pruned materials cut into small pieces and leftover grass clippings and fall leaves. Grass clippings should be left on the lawn for the most part, but you can collect them every couple of weeks to add to the pile.

Similarly, some of your fallen leaves should be chopped up with a mulching mower and left on the lawn; some can be collected and used directly as mulch under shrubs and on flowerbeds; and the remainder can be composted. Many gardeners collect leaves from their neighbors, store the leaves in plastic bags and add them to their compost pile over the following year.

Fruit and vegetable scraps from the kitchen may be added to the pile as well, but they may attract small animals. Always avoid putting weed seeds and diseased or pest-ridden plants into your compost pile, or you risk spreading problems throughout your entire garden.

After a season or two, the passive pile will have at the bottom a layer of pure black gold, looking much like the leaf mold found in the woods. That is your finished compost. You get to it by moving the top of the pile aside. Spreading out the

An active (hot) compost bin

finished compost on the surface of your beds will do good things for the soil. Because compost is usually in short supply, many gardeners just use it as an amendment when planting seedlings, perennials and small shrubs.

Many municipalities now recycle yard wastes into compost that is made available to residents. Contact your local government office to see if this valuable resource is available.

Finished compost

Selecting Perennials

PERENNIALS CAN BE PURCHASED or started from seed. Plants purchased in quart or gallon containers usually begin flowering the same year they are planted, while plants started from seed may take two growing seasons to flower. Starting plants from seed is more economical if you want large numbers of plants. (Find out how to start seeds in the section on propagating perennials, p. 42.)

Among the many sources for plants and seeds are garden centers, mail-order catalogs and friends and neighbors. A number of garden societies promote the exchange of seeds, and many public gardens sponsor plant sales in spring and fall. Gardening clubs are also a great source of rare and unusual plants. Get your perennials from a reputable source and be sure they are not diseased or pest-ridden.

Perennials may be sold in two forms. **Potted** perennials are actively growing and have probably been raised in the pot. **Bare-root** perennials usually come in a bag of moist sawdust or peat moss. They are sold dormant and no new growth should be visible, though some of the previous year's growth may be evident.

Potted perennials are a good choice because you can usually tell whether the plants are healthy. If the leaves appear to be chewed or damaged, or if they are an unhealthy color, check carefully for diseases or insects before you purchase the plant. If a plant is diseased, do not purchase it. If you find insects on the plant you may not want to purchase it, but if you do, it's important to deal with any problems before you transplant to avoid spreading the pest in your garden.

Potted plants come in many sizes, and although a larger plant may appear more mature, a smaller one will suffer less from the shock of being transplanted. Most perennials grow quickly once they are planted in the garden, so the initial size won't matter too much. Select plants that seem to be a good size for the pot they are in. When tapped lightly out of the pot, the roots should be visible and white. Pot-bound plants with roots that are winding and twisting around the inside of the pot have a more difficult time becoming established.

Once you get your potted plants home, water them if they are dry and keep them in a lightly shaded location until you are ready to plant them. Remove and discard any damaged growth. Try to plant your new perennials into the garden as soon as possible.

Bare-root plants are most commonly sold through mail order, because they are less expensive to ship, but some are available in stores, usually in the spring. It can be difficult to tell whether a bare-root plant is healthy or not. If the mail-order company is reputable, the plants will probably be healthy. Bare-root plants purchased from

Plant on left is rootbound, plant on right healthy.

stores, though, may not have been kept in ideal conditions and may take a long time to establish, if they establish at all. If you find that a plant you want is available in only this form, be careful to choose roots that are dormant and show no sign of top growth. Plants that have started growing may have too little energy to recover after trying to grow in the stressful conditions of a plastic bag.

Cut off any damaged parts of the roots with a very sharp knife. Bare-root perennials need to be planted more quickly than potted plants because they will dehydrate quickly out of soil. Soak the roots in lukewarm water and plant them either directly in the garden or into pots with good-quality potting soil until they can be moved to the garden.

It may be difficult to distinguish the top from the bottom of some bare-root plants. Usually there is a telltale dip or stub from which the above-ground parts previously grew. If you can't find any distinguishing characteristics, lay the root on its side and the plant will send the roots down and the shoots up.

Planting Perennials

ONCE YOU HAVE YOUR GARDEN PLANNED, the soil well prepared and the perennials purchased, it is time to plant. If your perennials have identification tags, be sure to poke them into the soil next to the new transplants. Next spring, when most of your perennial bed is nothing but a few stubs of green, the tags will help you with identification and remind you that there is indeed a plant in that bare patch of soil.

As well, keep a diagram of where you have planted everything. The diagram will help when tags are lost, moved or faded.

Plants should be spaced according to their anticipated spread. Overcrowded plants will grow poorly.

Potted Perennials

Perennials in pots are convenient because you can space them out across the bed or rearrange them before you start to dig. Once you have the collection organized to your satisfaction, you can begin planting. Do not unpot the plant until you have dug its hole because roots dry out quickly.

To plant potted perennials, start by digging a hole about the width and depth of the pot. Remove the perennial from the pot. If the pot is small enough, you can hold your hand across the top of the pot letting your fingers straddle the stem of the plant, and then turn it upside down. Never pull on the stem or leaves to get a plant out of a pot. It is better to cut a difficult pot off rather than risk damaging the plant. Tease a few roots out of the soil ball to get the plant growing in the right direction. If the roots have become densely wound around the inside of the pot, cut into the root mass with a sharp knife to encourage new growth into the surrounding soil. The process of cutting into the bottom half of the root ball and spreading the two halves of the mass outward like wings is called 'butterflying the roots' and is an effective way to promote fast growth of pot-bound perennials.

Place the plant into the prepared hole. It should be planted at the same level that it was at in the pot. Fill the soil in around the roots and firm it down. Water the plant well as soon as you have planted it, and water regularly until it has become established. After watering check the crown to be sure it is still at the proper level. If the plant sits too low in the ground, it may rot when rain collects around the crown. If it sits too high, the shoulders of the root ball may be exposed as the soil settles and the plant will dry out and die.

Support plant as you remove pot (above photos).

Loosen rootball before planting.

Bare-root Perennials

During planting, bare-root perennials should not be spaced out across the bed unless you previously planted them in temporary pots. Roots dry out very quickly if you leave them lying about waiting to be planted. If you want to visualize your spacing, poke sticks into the ground or put rocks or pots down to represent the locations of your perennials.

If you have been keeping your bare-root perennials in potting soil, you may find that the roots have not grown enough to knit the soil together and that all the soil falls away from the root when you remove it from the pot. Don't be concerned. Simply follow the regular root-planting instructions described in the next section. If the soil does hold together, plant the root the way you would a potted perennial.

The type of hole you need to dig depends on the type of roots the perennial has. Plants with **fibrous roots** need a mound of soil in the center of the planting hole over which the roots can spread out evenly. The hole should be dug as deep as the longest roots. Mound the soil into the center of the hole up to ground level. Spread the roots out around the mound and cover them with loosened soil. If you are adding just one or two plants and do not want to prepare an entire bed, dig a hole twice as wide and deep as the root ball and amend the soil with organic fertilizer, such as composted manure mixed with sphagnum peat moss.

Plants with a **taproot** need a hole that is narrow and about as deep as the root is long. The job is easily done with the help of a trowel: open up a suitable hole, tuck the root into it and fill it in again with the soil around it. If you can't tell which end is up, plant the root on its side.

Some plants have roots that appear to be taproots, but the shoot seems to be growing from the side of the root, rather than upwards from one end. These roots are actually modified stems called **rhizomes**. Iris roots are rhizomes. Rhizomes should be planted horizontally in a shallow hole and covered with soil.

In most cases, you should try to get the crown at or just above soil level and loosen the surrounding soil in the planting hole. Keep the roots thoroughly watered until the plants are well established.

Whether the plants are potted or bare-root, give them some time to recover from the stress of planting. In the first month, you will need only to water the plant regularly, weed around it and watch for pests. An organic mulch spread on the bed around your plants will keep in moisture and control weeds.

If you have prepared your beds properly, you probably won't have to fertilize in the first year. If you choose to fertilize, wait until your new plants have started healthy new growth, and apply only a weak fertilizer to avoid damaging the sensitive new roots.

Planters

Perennials can also be grown in planters for compact displays that can be moved about the garden. Planters can be used on patios or decks, in gardens with very poor soil or in yards where children and pets might destroy a traditional perennial bed. Many perennials, such as hostas and daylilies, can grow in the same container without any fresh potting soil for five or six years. Be sure, though, to fertilize and water perennials in planters more often than those growing in the ground. Dig your finger deep into the soil around the perennial to make sure it needs water. Too much water in a planter causes root rot.

Always use a good soil-less potting mix intended for containers. Garden soil quickly loses its structure and becomes a solid lump in a container, preventing air, water and roots from penetrating into the soil. Plants will never thrive in a container if planted in soil from the garden.

When designing a planter garden, you can either keep one type of perennial in each planter and display many planters together, or mix different perennials in large planters along with annuals and bulbs. The latter choice results in a dynamic bouquet of flowers and foliage. Keep the tall upright perennials such as yarrows in the center of the planter, the rounded or bushy types such as colorful coral bells and ajugas around the sides and low-growing or draping perennials such as dead nettles at the edges. Perennials that have long bloom times or attractive foliage work well in planters.

Mixed container planting

Choose hardy perennials that can tolerate difficult conditions. Plants in planters are exposed to extremes of our variable weather—baking hot in summer and freezing cold in winter. Plants will dry out quickly in hot weather and become waterlogged after a couple of rainy days. Not all perennials are tough enough to survive in these extreme conditions. Some of the more invasive perennial species are good choices, because their spread is controlled and they are very tough to kill.

Perennials in planters are more susceptible to winter damage because the exposed sides of the container provide little insulation against fluctuations in temperature.

The container itself may even crack when exposed to a deep freeze. Don't despair—you can move the planter to a sheltered spot in winter. Most perennials do require some cold in winter in order to flower the next year, so find a spot that is cold but provides some shelter. An unheated garage or enclosed porch is a good place, and even your garden shed will offer plants more protection than they would get sitting in the great outdoors, exposed to the elements on all sides. Just check them occasionally and water sparingly if the weather stays above freezing, to be sure the soil does not dry out completely.

You can try insulating large containers before planting perennials. Use house-insulation styrofoam or the 'peanut' or 'popcorn' type of packing material used to protect items in the mail. A layer of insulating material at the bottom and around the insides of the planter will protect the soil from freezing and thawing in winter and from excessive heat in summer; just make sure that water can drain freely from the container. This technique is useful for high-rise dwellers with balcony gardens.

Small pots are difficult to insulate and their size makes them even more vulnerable to the elements. If you don't have space for your pots in a shed or other sheltered area, you can bury them in the garden for the winter. Look for an open space in a flowerbed, perhaps where your annuals were growing, and dig a hole deep enough to allow you to sink the container up to its rim.

If space is a problem, remove the perennials from the planter and plant them out directly for the winter, then re-pot them the following spring. Too much potting and re-potting may take a toll on plants, though, so you may wish to leave the plants in the garden and start with new plants for your planters in spring.

Perennials for Planters

Candytuft
Catmint
Daylily
Dead Nettle
Goat's Beard
Hardy Geranium
Hosta
Lady's Mantle
Obedient Plant
Pincushion Flower
Pinks
Sedum
Speedwell
Yarrow

Lady's Mantle

Caring for Perennials

MANY PERENNIALS REQUIRE LITTLE CARE, but all benefit from a few maintenance basics. Weeding, mulching, watering, pruning and deadheading are a few of the chores that, when done on a regular basis, keep major work to a minimum.

Weeding

Controlling weeds is one of the most important things you will have to do in your garden. Weeds compete with your perennials for light, nutrients and space. Weeds can also harbor pests and diseases. Try to prevent weeds from germinating by mulching with 3–4" of organic material. If they do still germinate, pull them out while they are still small and before they have a chance to flower, set seed and start a whole new generation of problems.

Weeds can be pulled out by hand or with a hoe. Quickly scuffing across the soil surface with the hoe will pull out small weeds and sever larger ones from their roots.

Mulched garden

Mulching

Mulches are an important gardening tool. They prevent weed seeds from germinating by blocking out the light. As well, soil temperatures remain more consistent and more moisture is retained under a layer of mulch. Mulch also prevents soil erosion and compaction during heavy rain or strong winds.

Organic mulches include compost, bark chips, shredded leaves and grass clippings. Organic mulches are desirable because they improve the soil and release nutrients as they break down.

In spring, spread a couple of inches of mulch over your perennial beds around your plants. Keep the area immediately around the crown or stem of each plant clear. Mulch that is too close to your plants can trap moisture and prevent good air circulation, encouraging disease. If the layer of mulch disappears into the soil over the summer, replenish it.

Lay a fresh layer of mulch, up to 4" thick, once the ground freezes in fall to protect the plants over the winter. This mulch is particularly important if you live in an area of Michigan where you can't depend on a consistent layer of snow. You can also cover the plants themselves with dry material such as chopped straw, pine needles or shredded leaves. Make sure, though, that the ground has frozen before covering plants, because they may rot if they are covered too soon.

Keep in mind that as the ground freezes, so too may your pile of potential mulch, making it difficult to spread. One solution is to cover most of the bed with mulch, leaving only the plants exposed, before the ground freezes. Put extra mulch, needed to cover the plants, in a large plastic bag or your wheelbarrow and put it somewhere that will take longer to freeze, perhaps in your garage or the garden shed. Once the ground is completely frozen, you will have a supply of unfrozen mulch that you can use to cover the plants.

In late winter or early spring, when the weather starts to warm, pull the mulch layer off the plants and see if they have started growing. If they have, you can pull the mulch back, but keep it nearby in case you need it again to protect the tender new growth from a late frost.

Watering

Watering is another basic of perennial care. Once established, many perennials need little supplemental watering if they have been planted in their preferred conditions and are given a moisture-retaining mulch. Though the general rule is to water thoroughly and infrequently, some perennials will not survive unless their soil is kept constantly moist. Planting perennials with similar water requirements together makes watering easier. When you do water, make sure the water penetrates several inches into the soil. Installing soaker hoses in your perennial beds is one of the most efficient ways to water.

Fertilizing

If you prepare your beds well and add compost to them each spring, you should not need to add extra fertilizer. If you have a limited amount of compost, you can mix a slow-release fertilizer into the soil around your perennials in spring. Some plants, such as delphiniums, are heavy feeders that need additional supplements throughout the growing season.

Many organic and chemical fertilizers are available at garden centers. Be sure to use no more than the recommended quantity because too much fertilizer will do more harm than good. Roots can be burned by fertilizer that is applied in high concentrations. Problems are more likely to be caused by chemical fertilizers because they are more concentrated than organic fertilizers. Fresh manure, though, will also cause a fertilizer burn if it contacts roots directly. Make sure to use only well-rotted manure in the garden.

Grooming

Many perennials will benefit from a bit of grooming. Resilient plants, plentiful blooms and neat, compact growth are the signs of a well-groomed garden. Thinning, pinching, disbudding and deadheading plants are techniques used to enhance the beauty of a perennial garden. The methods are simple, but you may have to experiment in order to get the right effect in your own garden.

Thinning is done to clump-forming perennials like black-eyed Susans, Purple Coneflower, phloxes or Bergamot early in the year, when shoots have just emerged. These plants develop a dense clump of stems that allows very little air or light into the center of the plant. Remove one-third to one-half of the shoots when they first emerge. This removal will increase air circulation and prevent diseases such as powdery mildew. The increased

light will also encourage more compact growth and more flowers. Throughout the growing season, thin any growth that is weak, diseased or growing in the wrong direction.

Pinching or **trimming** perennials is a simple procedure, but timing it correctly and achieving just the right look can be tricky. Early in the year, before the flower buds have appeared, trim the plant to encourage new side shoots. Remove the tip and some stems of the plant just above a leaf or pair of leaves. This can be done stem by stem, but if you have a lot of plants you can trim off the tops with your hedge shears to one-third of the height you expect the plants to reach. The growth that begins to emerge can be pinched again. Beautiful layered effects can be achieved by staggering the trimming times by a week or two.

Give plants enough time to set buds and flower. Continual pinching will encourage very dense growth but also delay flowering. Most spring-flowering plants cannot be pinched back or they will not flower. Early-summer and mid-summer bloomers should be pinched only once, as early in the season as possible. Late-summer and fall bloomers can be pinched several times but should be left alone after June. Don't pinch the plant if flower buds have formed—it may not have enough energy or time left in the year to develop a new set of buds. Experimenting and keeping detailed notes will improve the timing of your pinching skills.

Shasta Daisy

re-seeding and helps prevent the spread of pests and diseases. The flowers can be pinched off by hand or snipped off with hand pruners. Bushy plants that have many tiny flowers, and particularly ones that have a short bloom period, such as Basket-of-gold, can be more aggressively pruned back with garden shears once they are finished flowering. In some cases, as with Creeping Phlox, shearing will promote new growth and possibly even a second flush of blooms later in the season.

Perennials to Pinch Early in the Season
Artemisia
Aster
Bergamot
Black-eyed Susan
Catmint
Chrysanthemum
Mallow
Purple Coneflower
Rose Mallow
Sedum 'Autumn Joy'
Shasta Daisy

Perennials to Shear Back after Blooming
Basket-of-gold
Catmint
Candytuft
Creeping Phlox
Bellflower
Dead Nettle
Golden Marguerite
Hardy Geranium
Sweet Woodruff
Thyme
Yarrow

Disbudding is the removal of some flower buds to encourage the remaining ones to produce larger flowers. This technique is popular with peony growers.

Deadheading, the removal of spent flowers, can serve several purposes. It prolongs blooming, keeps plants looking tidy, prevents

Golden Marguerite

Deadheading is not necessary for every plant. Some plants have attractive seedheads that will provide interest in the garden over the winter. As well, by leaving some of the seedheads of short-lived plants in place, you encourage re-seeding and cultivate new generations to replace the old plants. Hollyhock is one example of a short-lived perennial that often re-seeds. In some cases the self-sown seedlings do not possess the attractive features of the parent plant. Deadheading may be required in these cases.

Deadheading asters

Poppy and other seedheads (above),
Cardinal Flower (below)

Perennials with Interesting Seedheads
Astilbe
Goat's Beard
Meadowsweet
Oriental Poppy
Purple Coneflower
Russian Sage
Sedum 'Autumn Joy'

Perennials That Self-seed
Ajuga*
Bleeding Heart*
Cardinal Flower
Foxglove
Hollyhock*
Lady's Mantle
Mallow
Pinks
Rose Campion
Sundrops
(*variable seedlings)

Staking

Staking, the use of poles or wires to hold plants erect, can often be avoided by astute thinning and pinching, but a few plants always need a bit of support to look their best. Three types of stakes are used for the different growth habits that need support.

Plants that develop tall spikes, such as Hollyhock, delphiniums and some foxgloves, require each spike to be staked individually. A strong, narrow pole such as a bamboo stick can be pushed into the ground early in the year and the spike tied to the stake as it grows. A forked branch can also be used to support single-stemmed plants.

Many plants, such as peonies, get a bit top-heavy as they grow and tend to flop over once they reach a certain height. A wire hoop, sometimes called a peony ring, is the most unobtrusive way to hold up such a plant. When the plant is young, the legs of the peony ring are pushed into the ground around it and as the plant grows up, it is supported by the wire ring. At the same time, the bushy growth hides the ring. Wire tomato cages can also be used to support these types of plants.

Other plants, like coreopsis, form a floppy tangle of stems. These plants can be given a bit of support with twiggy branches inserted into the ground around young plants; the plants then grow up into the twigs. This method of support is called pea staking.

Some people consider stakes unsightly no matter how hidden they seem to be. You can do a few

Spiral stakes

things to reduce the need for staking. First, don't assume a plant will do better in a richer soil than is recommended. Very rich soil causes many plants to produce weak, leggy growth that is prone to falling over. Similarly, a plant that likes full sun will become stretched out and leggy if grown in the shade. Second, try combining different plants that can give each other some support. Mix in plants that have a more stable structure between the plants that need support. The weaker plants may still fall over slightly, but only as far as their neighbors will allow. Third, thin and pinch as recommended, to encourage stronger growth that is less likely to fall over. Finally, look for compact varieties that are available for many plants and don't require staking.

Propagating Perennials

LEARNING TO PROPAGATE your own perennials is an interesting and challenging aspect of gardening that can save you money, but it also requires time and space. Seeds, cuttings and division are the three methods of increasing your perennial population. Each method has advantages and disadvantages.

A cold frame will often come in handy regardless of which methods of propagation you use. A cold frame can be used to protect tender plants over the winter, to start vegetable seeds early in spring, to harden off plants before moving them to the garden, to protect fall-germinating seedlings and young cuttings or divisions, and to start seeds that need a cold treatment. This mini-greenhouse structure is built so that ground level on the inside of the cold frame is lower than on the outside. The angled, hinged lid is fitted with glass. The soil around the outside of the cold frame insulates the plants inside. The lid lets light in, so that the frame collects some heat during the day, and it prevents rain from damaging tender plants. If the interior gets too hot, the lid can be raised for ventilation.

A hot frame is insulated and has heating coils in the floor to prevent the soil from freezing or to maintain a constant soil temperature for germinating seeds or rooting cuttings.

Seeds

Starting perennials from seed is a great way to propagate a large number of plants at a relatively low cost. Seeds can be purchased or collected from your own or a friend's garden. The work involved in growing plants from seed is worth it when you see plants you raised from tiny seedlings finally begin to flower.

Seeding has some limitations. Some cultivars and varieties are hybrids that don't pass on their desirable traits to their offspring. Other perennials take a very long time to germinate, if they germinate at all, and an even longer time to grow to flowering size. Many perennials, however, grow easily from seed and flower within a year or two of being transplanted into the garden.

Specific propagation information is given for each plant in this book,

Shade cloth over cold frame

but there are a few basic rules for starting all seeds. Some seeds can be started directly in the garden, but it is easier to control temperature and moisture levels and to provide a sterile environment if you start the seeds indoors. Seeds can be started in pots or, if you need a lot of plants, flats. Use a sterile soil mix intended for starting seeds. The soil will generally need to be kept moist but not soggy. Most seeds germinate in moderately warm temperatures of about 57–70° F.

Many seed-starting supplies are available at garden centers; only some of these supplies are really necessary. Seed-tray dividers are useful. These dividers, often called plug trays or cell packs, are made of plastic and prevent the roots of seedlings from tangling with the roots of the other plants and then being disturbed when seedlings are transplanted. Heating coils or pads can also be useful. Placed under the pots or flats, they keep the soil at a constant temperature.

Fill your pot or seed tray with the soil mix and firm it down slightly—not too firmly or the soil will not drain. Wet the soil before planting

Prepared seed tray

Using folded paper to plant small seeds (above)

Spray bottle provides gentle mist (center); filling cell packs (below)

your seeds because they may wash into clumps if the soil is watered after the seeds are planted. Large seeds can be placed individually and spaced out in pots or trays. If you have dividers for your trays, you can plant one or two seeds per section. Small seeds may have to be sprinkled in a bit more randomly. Fold a sheet of paper in half and place the small seeds in the crease. Gently tap the underside of the fold to bounce or roll the seeds off the paper in a controlled manner. Some seeds are so tiny that they look like dust. These seeds can be mixed with a small quantity of very fine sand and spread on the soil surface. These tiny seeds may not need to be covered with any more soil. The medium-sized seeds can be lightly covered, and the larger seeds can be pressed into the soil and then lightly covered. Do not cover seeds that need to be exposed to light in order to germinate; these types of seeds are indicated as such in the plant descriptions later in the book.

Be sure to plant only one type of seed in each pot or flat. Each species has a different rate of germination and the germinated seedlings will require different conditions than the seeds.

Water the seeds using a very fine spray if the soil starts to dry out. A hand-held spray bottle will moisten the soil without disturbing the seeds. To help keep the environment moist, you can place pots inside clear plastic bags. Change the bag or turn it inside out once condensation starts to build up and drip. Plastic bags can be held above the plants with stakes or wires poked in around the edges of the pot. Many seed trays come with clear plastic covers that can be placed over the flats to keep the moisture in. The plastic can be removed once the seeds have germinated.

Seeds generally do not require a lot of light in order to germinate, so pots or trays can be kept in a warm, out-of-the-way place. Once the seeds have germinated, they can be placed in a bright location but out of direct sun. Plants should be transplanted to individual pots once they have three or four true leaves. True leaves are the ones that look like the mature leaves. (The first one or two leaves are the seed leaves, or cotyledons.) Plants in plug trays can be left until neighboring leaves start to touch each other. At this point the plants are competing for light and should be transplanted to individual pots.

Young seedlings do not need to be fertilized. Fertilizer causes seedlings to produce soft, spindly growth that is susceptible to attack by insects and diseases. The seed itself provides all the nutrition the seedling will need. A fertilizer diluted to one-quarter or one-half strength can be used once seedlings have four or five true leaves.

All seedlings are susceptible to a problem called damping off, which is caused by soil-borne fungi. An afflicted seedling looks as though someone has pinched the stem at soil level, causing the plant to topple over. The pinched area blackens and the seedling dies. Prevent damping off by using sterile soil mix, by maintaining good air circulation and by watering from the bottom to keep soil evenly moist rather then soggy.

Many seeds will sprout easily as soon as they are planted, but some have protection devices that prevent them from germinating when conditions are not favorable or from germinating all at once. In the wild, such strategies improve the chances of survival, but you will have to lower the defenses of these types of seeds before they will germinate.

Delphinium

Perennials Easy to Start from Seed
Delphinium
Foxglove
Pinks
Hollyhock
Lady's Mantle
Rose Campion

Pinks

Seeds can be tricked into thinking the conditions are right for sprouting. Some thick-coated seeds can be soaked for a day or two in a glass of water to promote germination. The soaking mimics the beginning of the rainy season, which is when the plant would germinate in its natural environment. The water softens the seed coat and in some cases washes away the chemicals that have been inhibiting germination. Rose Mallow is an example of a plant with seeds that need to be soaked before they will germinate.

Other thick-coated seeds need to have their seed coats scratched to allow moisture to penetrate the seed coat and prompt germination. In nature, birds scratch the seeds with gravel in their craws and acid in their stomachs. Nick the seeds with a knife or gently rub them between two sheets of sandpaper. After scratching the seeds, leave them in a dry place for a day or so before planting, to allow them to prepare for germination before they are exposed to water. Anemones are plants with seeds that need their thick coats scratched.

Plants from northern climates often have seeds that wait until spring before they germinate. These seeds have to be exposed to cold

temperatures, to mimic winter, before they will germinate. Yarrows, bergenias and primroses have seeds that respond to cold treatment.

One method of cold treatment is to plant the seeds in a pot or tray and place them in the refrigerator for up to two months. Check the container regularly and don't allow the seeds to dry out. This method is fairly simple but not very practical if your refrigerator is as crowded as mine.

A less space consuming method is to mix the seeds with some moistened sand, peat or sphagnum moss. Place the mix in a sealable sandwich bag and pop it in the refrigerator for up to two months, again being sure the sand or moss doesn't dry out. The seeds can then be planted in the pot or tray. Spread the seeds in the moist sand or moss on the prepared surface and press it down gently.

As noted in certain species entries in this book, some plants have seeds that must be planted when they are freshly ripe. These seeds cannot be stored for long periods of time.

Mixing seeds with moist peat for cold treatment

Scratching seed coats with sandpaper

Cuttings

Cuttings are an excellent way to propagate varieties and cultivars that you really like but that don't come true from seed or don't produce seed at all. Each cutting will grow into an exact reproduction of the parent plant. Cuttings are taken from the stems of some perennials and from the basal growth, roots or rhizomes of others.

Stem cuttings are generally taken in spring and early summer. During this time plants produce a flush of fresh, new growth, either before or after flowering. Avoid taking cuttings from plants that are in flower.

Plants that are blooming or about to bloom are busy trying to reproduce; plants that are busy growing, by contrast, are already full of the right hormones to promote quick root growth. If you do take cuttings from plants that are flowering, be sure to remove the flowers and the buds in order to divert the plant's energy back into growing.

Cuttings need to be kept in a warm, humid place to root, which makes them prone to fungal diseases. Providing proper sanitation and encouraging quick rooting will increase the survival rate of your cuttings, but be sure to plant a lot of them to make up for any losses.

A) Removing lower leaves
B) Dipping in rooting hormone

C) Firming cutting into soil
D) Healthy roots

Coreopsis (above)

Bleeding Heart (center), Yarrow (below)

Perennials to Start from Stem Cuttings

Artemisia
Aster
Basket-of-gold
Bellflower
Bleeding Heart
Candytuft
Catmint
Chrysanthemum
Coreopsis
Euphorbia
Penstemon
Pinks
Sedum 'Autumn Joy'
Speedwell
Thyme
Yarrow

Debate exists over what size cuttings should be. Some gardeners claim that smaller cuttings are more likely to root and to root more quickly. Other gardeners claim that larger cuttings develop more roots and become established more quickly once planted in the garden. You may wish to try different sizes to see what works best for you. A small cutting is about 1–2" long and a large cutting is about 4–6" long.

Size of cuttings is partly determined by the number of leaf nodes on the cutting. You will want at least three or four nodes on a cutting. The node is where the leaf joins the stem, and it is from here that the new roots will grow. The base of the cutting will be just below a node. Strip the leaves gently from the first and second nodes and plant them below the soil. The above-ground parts will grow from the nodes above the soil; keep the leaves in place on these nodes. Some plants have a lot of space between nodes, so that your cutting may be longer than the guideline ranges above. Other plants have almost no space at all between the nodes. Cut these plants according to the guidelines, and gently remove the leaves from the lower half of the cutting. Plants with closely spaced nodes often root quickly and abundantly.

Always use a sharp, sterile knife to take cuttings. Cuts should be made straight across the stem. Once you have stripped the leaves, you can dip the end of the cutting into a rooting-hormone powder intended for soft-wood cuttings. Sprinkle the powder onto a piece of paper and dip the cuttings into it. Discard any extra powder left on the paper to prevent the spread of disease. Tap or blow the extra powder off the cutting. Cuttings caked with rooting hormone are more likely to rot than to root, and they do not root any faster than those that are lightly dusted.

Your cuttings are now prepared for planting. The sooner you plant them, the better. The less water the cuttings lose, the less likely they are to wilt and the more quickly they will root. Cuttings can be planted in a similar manner to seeds. Use sterile soil mix, intended for seeds or cuttings, in pots or trays. You can also root cuttings in sterilized sand, perlite, vermiculite or a combination of the three. Firm the soil down and moisten it before you start planting. Poke a hole in the soil with a pencil or similar object, tuck the cutting in and gently firm the soil around it. Make sure the lowest

leaves do not touch the soil and that the cuttings are spaced far enough apart that adjoining leaves do not touch each other.

Use pots or trays that can be covered with plastic to keep in the humidity. If you are using a plastic bag to cover a pot, push stakes or wires into the soil around the edge of the pot so that the plastic will be held off the leaves. The rigid plastic lids that are available for trays may not be high enough to fit over cuttings, in which case you will have to use stakes and a plastic bag to cover the tray.

Keep the soil moist. A hand-held mister will gently moisten the soil without disturbing the cuttings. If the condensation becomes heavy, turn the bag inside out. A couple of holes poked in the bag will allow for some ventilation.

Keep the cuttings in a warm place, about 65–70° F, in bright indirect light. Most cuttings will require from one to four weeks to root. After two weeks, give the cutting a gentle tug. You will feel resistance if roots have formed. If the cutting feels as though it will easily pull out of the soil, gently push it back down and give it more time. New growth is also a good sign that your cutting has rooted. Some gardeners simply leave cuttings alone until they can see roots through the holes in the bottoms of the pots. Uncover cuttings once they have developed roots.

Apply a foliar feed when the cuttings are showing new leaf growth. Plants quickly absorb nutrients through the leaves; by using a foliar feed, you can avoid stressing the newly formed roots. Your local garden center should have foliar feeds and information about applying them. Your hand-held mister can be used to apply foliar feeds.

Once your cuttings have rooted and have had a chance to establish themselves, they can be potted individually. If you rooted several cuttings in one pot or tray, you may find that the roots have tangled together. If gentle pulling doesn't separate them, take the entire clump that is tangled together and try rinsing some of the soil away. This should free the roots enough for you to separate the plants.

Pot the young plants in a sterile potting soil. They can be moved into a sheltered area of the garden or a cold frame and grown in pots until they are large enough to outcompete

weeds in the garden. The plants may need some protection over the first winter. Keep them in the cold frame if they are still in pots, or give them an extra layer of mulch if they have been planted out.

Basal cuttings involve removing the new growth from the main clump and rooting it in the same manner as stem cuttings. Many plants send up new shoots or plantlets around their bases. Often, the plantlets will already have a few roots growing. These young plants develop quickly and may even grow to flowering size the first summer.

Treat these cuttings the same way you would stem cuttings. Use a sterile knife to cut out the new shoots. Ideally, plant the cuttings in sterile soil mix and give them humid conditions. Pot plants individually or place them in soft soil in the garden until new growth appears and roots have developed.

Perennials to Start from Basal Cuttings
Ajuga
Bellflower
Bergamot
Catmint
Daylily
Dead Nettle
Delphinium
Euphorbia
Hardy Geranium
Hens and Chicks
Hollyhock
Phlox
Pincushion Flower
Sedum

Sedum (above), Hens and Chicks (below)

Root cuttings can also be taken from some plants. Dandelions are well known for their ability to propagate this way: as most of us know, even the smallest piece of root left in the ground can sprout a new plant, foiling every attempt to eradicate dandelions from lawns and flowerbeds. But there are desirable perennials that share this ability.

Cuttings can be taken from the fleshy roots of certain perennials that do not propagate well from stem cuttings. These cuttings should be taken in early or mid-spring when the ground is just starting to warm up and the roots are about to break dormancy. At this time, the roots are full of nutrients, which the plants stored the previous summer and fall, and hormones are initiating growth. You may have to wet the soil around the plant so that you can loosen it enough to get to the roots.

The main difference between starting root cuttings and starting stem cuttings is that the root cuttings must be kept fairly dry, because they can rot very easily. Keep the roots just slightly moist while you are rooting them and keep track of which end is up. Roots must be planted in a vertical, not horizontal, position, with the part of the root that was closest to the parent plant at the top. There are different tricks people use to help them remember which end is up. One method is to cut straight across the tops and diagonally across the bottoms.

You do not want very young or very old roots. Very young roots are usually white and quite soft; very old roots tend to be tough and woody.

The roots you should use will be tan in color and still fleshy. To prepare a root, cut out the section you will be using with a sterile knife. Cut the root into pieces that are 1–2" long. Remove any side roots before planting the sections in pots or planting trays. You can use the same type of soil mix in the pots as you would for starting seeds and stem cuttings. Poke the pieces vertically into the soil and leave a tiny bit of the end poking up out of the soil. Remember to keep the pieces the right way up.

Keep the pots or trays in a warm place out of direct sunlight. Avoid overwatering them. They will send up new shoots once they have rooted and can be planted in the same manner as the stem cuttings (see p. 47).

Perennials to Start from Root Cuttings

Anemone
Black-eyed Susan
Bleeding Heart
Oriental Poppy
Phlox
Plume Poppy
Primrose

Black-eyed Susan

Rhizomes are the easiest root cuttings with which to propagate plants. Rhizomes are thick, fleshy modified stems that grow horizontally along the ground, just under the soil. A rhizome sends up new shoots periodically along its length, and in this way the plant spreads. It is easy to take advantage of this feature.

Dig up a length of rhizome when the plant is growing vigorously, usually in late spring or early summer. If you look at the rhizome closely, you will see that it appears to be growing in sections. The places where these sections join are the nodes. It is from these nodes that small, stringy feeder roots extend downwards and new shoots sprout upwards. You may even see small plantlets already starting.

Cut your chunk of rhizome into pieces. Each piece should have at least one node in it.

Fill a pot or planting tray to about 1" from the top of the container with perlite, vermiculite or seeding soil. Moisten the soil and let the excess water drain away. Lay the rhizome pieces flat on the top of the mix and barely cover them with more of the soil mix. If you leave a small bit of the top exposed to the light, it will encourage the shoots to sprout. The soil does not have to be kept wet; moisten the soil only when it dries out in order to avoid having your rhizome rot.

Once your rhizome cuttings have established themselves, they can be potted individually and grown from then on in the same manner as the stem cuttings (see p. 47).

Perennials to Start from Rhizomes
Bellflower
Bergenia
Hardy Geranium
Iris
Wild Ginger

Hardy Geranium

Iris

Division

Division is quite possibly the easiest way to propagate perennials. As most perennials grow, they form larger and larger clumps. Dividing this clump periodically will rejuvenate the plant, keep its size in check and provide you with more plants. If a plant you want is expensive, consider buying only one because within a few years you may have more than you can handle.

How often a perennial needs dividing or can be divided depends on the plant. Some perennials, like astilbes, need dividing almost every year to keep them vigorous, while others, like peonies, should never be divided because they dislike having their roots disturbed. Each perennial entry in this book gives recommendations for division.

You can watch for several signs that indicate a perennial may need dividing:

- the center of the plant has died out
- the plant is no longer flowering as profusely as it did in previous years
- the plant is encroaching on the growing space of other plants sharing the bed.

It is relatively easy to divide perennials. Begin by digging up the entire clump and knocking any large clods of soil away from the rootball. The clump can then be split into several pieces. A small plant with fibrous roots can be torn into sections by hand. A large plant can be pried apart with a pair of garden forks inserted back to back into the clump. Plants with thicker tuberous or rhizomatous roots can be cut into sections with a sharp,

Digging up perennials for division (above & center)

Clump of stems, roots & crowns (below)

Pulling clump apart

Cutting apart and dividing tuberous perennials

sterile knife. In all cases, cut away any old sections that have died out and re-plant only the newer, more vigorous sections.

Once your original clump is divided into sections, re-plant one or two of them into the original location. Take this opportunity to work organic matter into the soil where the perennial was growing before re-planting it. The other sections can be moved to new spots in the garden or potted and given as gifts to gardening friends and neighbors. Get the sections back into the ground as quickly as possible to prevent the exposed roots from drying out. Plan where you are going to plant your divisions and have the spots prepared before you start digging anything up. Plant your perennial divisions in pots if you aren't sure where to put them all. Water the new transplants thoroughly and keep them well watered until they have re-established themselves.

The larger the sections of the division, the more quickly they will re-establish and grow to blooming size again. For example, a perennial divided into four sections will bloom sooner than the same plant divided into ten sections. Very small divisions may benefit from being planted in pots until they are bigger and better able to fend for themselves in the garden.

Newly planted divisions will need extra care and attention when they are first planted. They will need regular watering and, for the first few days, shade from direct sun. A light covering of burlap or damp newspaper should be sufficient to shelter them for this short period. Divisions that have been planted in pots should be moved to a shaded location.

There is some debate about the best time to divide perennials. Some gardeners prefer to divide perennials while they are dormant, whereas others feel that perennials establish themselves more quickly if divided when they are growing vigorously. Still others decide when to divide on the basis of when the plant blooms. These gardeners divide fall bloomers in spring, and divide spring and summer bloomers after they bloom or in fall. When dividing in fall, a general rule is to allow six weeks for the plant to become established before the ground freezes. You may wish to experiment with dividing at different times of the year to see what works best for you.

Perennials That Don't Like Division
Basket-of-gold
Butterfly Weed
Clematis
Columbine
Euphorbia
False Indigo
Meadow Rue
Monkshood
Peony
Pinks
Sea Holly

False Indigo (above)

Columbine (center), Peony (below)

Problems & Pests

PERENNIAL GARDENS ARE BOTH AN ASSET and a liability when it comes to pests and diseases. Perennial beds often contain a mixture of different plant species. Many insects and diseases attack only one species of plant, so mixed beds make it difficult for pests and diseases to find their preferred hosts and establish a population. At the same time, because the plants are in the same spot for many years, problems that do develop can become permanent. Yet, if allowed, beneficial insects, birds and other pest-devouring organisms can also develop permanent populations.

For many years pest control meant spraying or dusting, with the goal to try to eliminate every pest in the garden. A more moderate approach is advocated today, in which the goal is to maintain problems at levels where only negligible damage is done.

Chemicals are a last resort because they often do more harm than good.

They can endanger the gardener and his or her family and they kill the good organisms along with the bad, leaving the garden vulnerable to even worse attacks.

A responsible pest-management program has four components. Cultural controls are the most important. Physical controls should be attempted next, followed by biological controls. Chemical controls should be used only when the first three possibilities have been exhausted.

Cultural controls are the gardening techniques you use in the day-to-day care of your garden. Growing perennials in the conditions they prefer and keeping your soil healthy with plenty of organic matter are just two of the cultural controls you can use to keep pests manageable in your garden. Choose resistant varieties of perennials that are not prone to problems. Space perennials so that they have good air circulation around them and are not stressed from competing for light, nutrients and space. Remove plants from the garden if they are constantly decimated by the same pests every year. Remove and destroy diseased foliage and prevent the spread of disease by keeping your gardening tools clean and by tidying up fallen leaves and dead plant matter at the end of the growing season.

Physical controls are generally used to combat insect problems. An example of such a control is picking insects off plants by hand, which is not as daunting a solution as it seems if you catch the problem when it is just beginning. Other physical controls include barriers that stop insects from getting to the plant, and traps that either catch or confuse insects. Physical control of diseases often necessitates removing the infected plant or parts of it, in order to prevent the spread of the problem.

Butterflies in the garden add color and charm

Tidying up the garden (below)

Frogs eat many insect pests.

Biological controls make use of populations of natural predators. Such animals as birds, snakes, frogs, spiders, lady beetles and certain bacteria can all help keep pest populations at a manageable level. Try to encourage these creatures to take up permanent residence in your garden. A birdbath and birdfeeder will encourage birds to enjoy your yard and feed on a wide variety of insect pests. Many beneficial insects are probably already living in your garden, and you can encourage them to stay by planting appropriate food sources. Many beneficial insects eat nectar from flowers such as yarrow.

Chemical controls should rarely be necessary in a perennial garden, but if you feel you must use them, some 'organic' options are available. Organic sprays are no less dangerous than chemical ones, but they are made using natural products and eventually break down into harmless compounds. The main drawback to using any chemicals is that they may also kill the beneficial insects you have been trying to attract to your garden. Organic chemicals should be available at local garden centers. Appy them carefully in the manufacturer's recommended amounts, and use them to combat only the pests listed on the package. Proper and early identification of problems is vital in finding a quick solution.

Whereas cultural, physical, biological and chemical controls are all possible defenses against insects, diseases generally must be controlled culturally. Prevention is often the only hope: once a plant has been infected, it should probably be destroyed to prevent spread of the disease. This is particularly true for highly infectious, deadly diseases such as blight. Less severe diseases, such as powdery mildew, may be controllable using less extreme measures.

Glossary of Pests & Diseases

Aphids

Tiny, pear-shaped insects, winged or wingless; green, black, brown, red or gray. Cluster along stems, on buds and on leaves. Suck sap from plants; cause distorted or stunted growth. Sticky honeydew forms on surfaces and encourages sooty mold growth. Woolly adelgids are a type of aphid. **What to Do:** Squish small colonies by hand; dislodge with brisk water spray; encourage predatory insects and birds that feed on aphids; spray serious infestations with insecticidal soap or neem oil according to package directions.

Caterpillar eating flowers (above),
green aphids (center)

Aster Yellows

see Viruses

Beetles

Many types and sizes; usually rounded in shape with hard, shell-like outer wings covering membranous inner wings. Some beetles are beneficial, e.g., ladybird beetles ('ladybugs'); others, e.g., June beetles, leaf skeletonizers and weevils,

Beneficial ladybird beetle larva (below)

Spittle mass (above) can be washed away; leaf miner tunnels (below)

coffee can half filled with soapy water (soap prevents them from floating and climbing out).

Blight
Fungal diseases, many types; e.g., leaf blight, needle blight, snow blight. Leaves, stems and flowers blacken, rot and die.
What to Do: Thin stems to improve air circulation; keep mulch away from base of plants; remove debris from garden at end of growing season. Remove and destroy infected plant parts.

Bugs (True Bugs)
Small insects, up to $1/2$" long; green, brown, black or brightly colored and patterned. Many beneficial; a few pests, such as lace bugs, pierce plants to suck out sap. Toxins may be injected that deform plants; sunken areas left where pierced; leaves rip as they grow; leaves, buds and new growth may be dwarfed and deformed.
What to Do: Remove debris and weeds from around plants in fall to destroy overwintering sites. Spray plants with insecticidal soap or neem oil according to package directions.

Case Bearers
see Caterpillars

Caterpillars
Larvae of butterflies, moths, sawflies. Include bagworms, budworms, case bearers, cutworms, leaf rollers, leaf tiers, loopers. Chew foliage and buds; can completely defoliate a plant if infestation severe.

eat plants. Larvae: see Borers, Grubs. Wide range of chewing damage: make small or large holes in or around margins of leaves; consume entire leaves or areas between leaf veins ('skeletonize'); may also chew holes in flowers. Some bark beetle species carry deadly plant diseases.
What to Do: Pick beetles off at night and drop them into an old

What to Do: Removal from plant is best control. Use high-pressure water and soap or pick caterpillars off small plants by hand. Control biologically using the naturally occurring soil bacterium *Bacillus thuringiensis* var. *kurstaki* or *B.t.* for short (commercially available), which breaks down gut lining of caterpillars.

Galls

Unusual swellings of plant tissues that may be caused by insects or diseases. Can affect leaves, buds, stems, flowers, fruit. Often a specific gall affects a single genus or species.
What to Do: Cut galls out of plant and destroy them. Galls caused by insects usually contain the insect's eggs and juvenile stages. Prevent such galls by controlling insect before it lays eggs; otherwise try to remove and destroy infected tissue before young insects emerge. Generally insect galls are more unsightly than damaging to plant. Galls caused by diseases often require destruction of plant. Avoid placing other plants susceptible to same disease in that location.

Grubs

Larvae of different beetles, commonly found below soil level; usually curled in C-shape. Body white or gray; head may be white, gray, brown or reddish. Problematic in lawns; may feed on roots of perennials. Plant wilts despite regular watering; may pull easily out of ground in severe cases.
What to Do: Toss any grubs found while digging onto a stone path,

Ladybird beetle

driveway, road or patio for birds to devour; apply parasitic nematodes or milky spore to infested soil (ask at your local garden center).

Leafhoppers & Treehoppers

Small, wedge-shaped insects; can be green, brown, gray or multi-colored. Jump around frantically when disturbed. Suck juice from plant leaves, cause distorted growth, carry diseases such as aster yellows.
What to Do: Encourage predators by planting nectar-producing species like yarrow. Wash insects off with strong spray of water; spray plants

Beneficial predatory ground beetle

Snail eating leaf

with insecticidal soap or neem oil according to package directions.

Leaf Miners

Tiny, stubby larvae of some butterflies and moths; may be yellow or green. Tunnel within leaves leaving winding trails; tunneled areas are lighter in color than rest of leaf. Unsightly rather than major health risk to plant. **What to Do:** Remove debris from area in fall to destroy overwintering sites; attract parasitic wasps with nectar plants such as yarrow. Remove and destroy all infected foliage; can sometimes squish by hand within leaf.

Leaf Rollers

see Caterpillars

Leaf Skeletonizers

see Beetles

Leaf Spot

Two common types: one caused by bacteria and one by fungi. *Bacterial:* small brown or purple spots grow to encompass entire leaves; leaves may drop. *Fungal:* black, brown or yellow spots; leaves wither; e.g., scab, tar spot. **What to Do:** Bacterial infection more severe; must remove entire plant. For fungal infection, remove and destroy infected plant parts. Sterilize removal tools; avoid wetting foliage or touching wet foliage; remove and destroy debris at end of growing season.

Mealybugs

Tiny crawling insects related to aphids; appear to be covered with white fuzz or flour. Sucking damage stunts and stresses plant. Excrete honeydew that promotes growth of sooty mold. **What to Do:** Remove by hand from smaller plants; wash plants with soap and water; wipe off with alcohol-soaked swabs; remove heavily infested leaves; encourage or introduce natural predators such as mealybug destroyer beetle and parasitic wasps; spray with insecticidal soap. Keep in mind larvae of mealybug destroyer beetles look like very large mealybugs.

Mildew

Two types, both caused by fungus, but with slightly different symptoms. *Downy mildew:* yellow spots on upper sides of leaves and downy fuzz on undersides; fuzz may be yellow, white or gray. *Powdery mildew:* white or gray powdery coating on leaf surfaces, doesn't brush off. **What to Do:** Choose resistant cultivars; space plants well; thin stems to encourage air circulation; tidy any debris in fall. Remove and destroy infected leaves or other parts.

Mites

Tiny, eight-legged relatives of spiders; do not eat insects, but may spin webs. Almost invisible to naked eye; red, yellow or green; usually found on undersides of plant leaves. Examples: bud mites, spider mites, spruce mites. Suck juice out of leaves. May see fine webbing on leaves and stems; may see mites moving on leaf undersides; leaves become discolored and speckled, then turn brown and shrivel up.
What to Do: Wash off with strong spray of water daily until all signs of infestation are gone; predatory mites available through garden centers; spray plants with insecticidal soap.

Mosaic

see Viruses

Nematodes

Tiny worms that give plants disease symptoms. One type infects foliage and stems; the other infects roots. *Foliar:* yellow spots that turn brown on leaves; leaves shrivel and wither; problem starts on lowest leaves and works up plant. *Root-knot:* plant is stunted, may wilt; yellow spots on leaves; roots have tiny bumps or knots.
What to Do: Mulch soil, add organic matter, clean up debris in fall, don't touch wet foliage of infected plants. Can add parasitic nematodes to soil. Remove infected plants in extreme cases.

Rot

Several different fungi that affect different parts of plant and can kill plant. *Crown rot:* affects base of plant, causing stems to blacken and fall over and leaves to yellow and wilt. *Root rot:* leaves yellow and plant wilts; digging up plant shows roots rotted away. *White rot:* a 'watery decay fungus' that affects any part of plant; cell walls appear to break down, releasing fluids.
What to Do: Keep soil well drained; don't damage plant if you are digging around it; keep mulches away from plant base. Destroy infected plant if whole plant affected.

Rust

Fungi. Pale spots on upper leaf surfaces; orange, fuzzy or dusty spots on leaf undersides. Examples: blister rust, hollyhock rust.
What to Do: Choose rust-resistant varieties and cultivars; avoid handling wet leaves; provide plant with good air circulation; clear up garden debris at end of season. Remove and destroy infected plant parts.

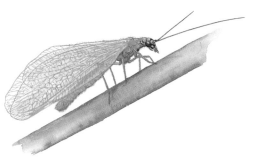

Green lacewings are beneficial predators in the garden.

Lygus bug feeding may disfigure flowers.

Scab
see Leaf Spot

Scale Insects
Tiny, shelled insects that suck sap, weakening and possibly killing plant or making it vulnerable to other problems. Once female scale insect has pierced plant with mouthpart, it is there for life. Juvenile scale insects are called crawlers.
What to Do: Wipe off with alcohol-soaked swabs; spray with water to dislodge crawlers; prune out heavily infested branches; encourage natural predators and parasites; spray dormant oil in spring before bud break.

Slugs & Snails
Both mollusks; slugs lack shells whereas snails have spiral shells. Can be up to 8" long, many smaller. Slimy, smooth skin; gray, green, black, beige, yellow or spotted. Leave large, ragged holes in leaves and silvery slime trails on and around plants.
What to Do: Attach strips of copper to wood around raised beds or to smaller boards inserted around susceptible groups of plants; slugs and snails get shocked if they try to cross copper surfaces. Pick off by hand in the evening and squish with boot or drop in can of soapy water. Spread wood ash or diatomaceous earth (available in garden centers) on ground around plants; it will pierce their soft bodies and dehydrate them. Slug baits containing iron phosphate (also available in garden centers) are not harmful to humans or animals and control slugs very well when used according to package directions. If slugs damaged garden last season, begin controls as soon as new green shoots appear in spring.

Sooty Mold
Fungus. Thin black film forms on leaf surfaces and reduces amount of light getting to leaf surfaces.
What to Do: Wipe mold off leaf surfaces; control insects like aphids, mealybugs, whiteflies (honeydew left on leaves encourages mold).

Tar Spot
see Leaf Spot

Thrips
Tiny, slender insects, difficult to see; may be visible if you disturb them by blowing gently on an infested flower. Yellow, black or brown; narrow, fringed wings. Suck juice out of plant cells, particularly in flowers and buds, causing mottled petals and leaves, dying buds, distorted and stunted growth.
What to Do: Remove and destroy infected plant parts; encourage native predatory insects with plants like yarrow; spray severe infestations with insecticidal soap or neem oil according to directions.

Viruses

Plant may be stunted and leaves and flowers distorted, streaked or discolored. Examples: aster yellows, mosaic virus, ringspot virus.
What to Do: Viral diseases in plants cannot be treated. Control disease-spreading insects, such as aphids, leafhoppers and whiteflies. Destroy infected plants.

Weevils
see Beetles

Whiteflies

Flying insects that flutter up into the air when plant is disturbed. Tiny, moth-like, white; live on undersides of plant leaves. Suck juice out of leaves, causing yellowed leaves and weakened plants; leave behind sticky honeydew on leaves, encouraging sooty mold growth.
What to Do: Destroy weeds where insects may live. Attract native predatory beetles and parasitic wasps with nectar plants like yarrow; spray severe cases with insecticidal soap. Can make a sticky flypaper-like trap by mounting tin can on stake; wrap can with yellow paper and cover with clear plastic bag smeared with petroleum jelly; replace bag when covered in flies.

Wilt

If watering doesn't help wilted plant, one of two wilt fungi may be at fault. *Fusarium wilt:* plant wilts, leaves turn yellow then die; symptoms generally appear first on one part of plant before spreading to other parts. *Verticillium wilt:* plant wilts; leaves curl up at edges; leaves

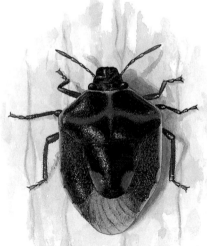

Harlequin bug is a garden pest.

turn yellow then drop off; plant may die.
What to Do: Both wilts difficult to control. Choose resistant plant varieties and cultivars; clean up debris at end of growing season. Destroy infected plants; solarize (sterilize) soil before re-planting (may help if entire bed of plants lost to these fungi)—contact local garden center for assistance.

Woolly Adelgids
see Aphids

Worms
see Caterpillars, Nematodes

You can make your own insecticidal soap at home. Mix 1 tsp. of mild dish detergent or pure soap (biodegradable options are available) with 1 qt. of water in a clean spray bottle. Spray the surfaces of your plants and rinse well within an hour of spraying to avoid foliage discoloration.

About This Guide

THE PERENNIALS IN THIS BOOK are organized alphabetically by their most familiar common names. Additional common names and scientific names appear after the primary reference. The illustrated **Flowers at a Glance** section at the beginning of the book allows you to become familiar with the different flowers quickly, and it will help you find a plant if you're not sure what it's called.

Clearly indicated at the beginning of each entry are height and spread ranges, flower colors, blooming times and hardiness zones. At the back of the book, you will find a **Quick Reference Chart** that summarizes different features and requirements of the plants; you will find this chart handy when planning diversity in your garden.

Each entry gives clear instructions for planting and growing the perennial, and recommends our favorite species and varieties. *Note:* Plant sizes and hardiness zones are given for each recommended species only if the ranges differ from those at the beginning of the entry. Keep in mind, too, that many more hybrids, cultivars and varieties are often available. Check with your local greenhouses or garden centers when making your selection.

Pests or diseases common to a plant, if any, are also listed for each entry. Consult the 'Problems & Pests' section of the introduction to find information on how to solve the common problems that can plague your plants.

The
Perennials
for Michigan

Ajuga
Bugleweed
Ajuga

Height: 4–12" **Spread:** 18–36" **Flower color:** purple, blue, pink, white; plant grown for foliage **Blooms:** late spring to early summer **Zones:** 3–8

GARDENERS WHO ONCE CONSIDERED these aggressive groundcovers passé are giving them a second look, thanks to the introduction of new cultivars that provide colorful foliage throughout the growing season. My favorite, the multi-colored 'Burgundy Glow,' combines silver, pink, bronze and soft green and makes a classy accent plant in shade gardens. 'Caitlin's Giant,' with its large, bronze leaves, lends interest as a foliage plant in containers or as a groundcover.

Planting

Seeding: Not recommended; foliage often reverts to green in seedlings

Planting out: Any time of year

Spacing: 12–18"

Growing

Ajugas develop the best leaf color in **partial or light shade** but tolerate full sun and full shade. The leaves may become scorched in direct sun. Any **well-drained** soil is suitable. Winter protection, such as a mulch, is recommended if snow cover isn't dependable in your garden. Divide these vigorous plants any time during the growing season.

Remove any new growth or seedlings that don't show the hybrid leaf coloring.

Tips

Ajugas make excellent groundcovers for difficult sites, such as exposed slopes and dense shade. They are also attractive groundcovers in shrub borders, where their dense growth will prevent the spread of all but the most tenacious weeds.

A. reptans with *Antirrhinum*

A. r. 'Chocolate Chip'

An ajuga syrup has been used to cure hangovers.

A. *reptans* cultivars

Ajuga reptans *is widely used in homeopathic remedies for throat and mouth irritations.*

If you plant ajugas next to a lawn, you may soon be calling them weeds. These plants can easily take over the lawn because they spread readily by stolons (above-ground shoots) and their low growth escapes the lawn-mower blades. The spread of ajugas may be somewhat controlled by the use of bed-edging materials. If an ajuga starts to take over, it is easy to rip out, and the soil it leaves behind will be soft and loose from the penetrating roots. Use an ajuga as a scout plant to send ahead and prepare the soil before you plant anything more particular in a shaded or woodland garden.

If you're not a stickler when it comes to edging beds, plant these aggressive growers in areas bordered by brick or cement. Close spacing and regular watering helps these plants spread quickly and fill in, preventing weeds from springing up among the groundcover.

Recommended

A. reptans is a low, quick-spreading groundcover about 6" tall and 18–24" in spread. 'Braunherz' ('Bronze Heart') is an excellent, purple-bronze cultivar with bright blue flowers. It remains compact and richly colored all year. 'Burgundy Glow' has variegated foliage in shades of bronze, green, white and pink. The habit is dense and compact.

'**Caitlin's Giant**' has large, bronze leaves. It bears short spikes of bright blue flowers in spring. '**Chocolate Chip**' has a low, creeping form, 6" tall and up to 36" in spread, with chocolaty bronze, teardrop-shaped leaves. It bears spikes of blue flowers in early summer. '**Multicolor**' ('Rainbow,' 'Tricolor') is a vigorous spreader. The bronze leaves feature splashes of pink and white. '**Variegata**' is dense and slow growing. The green leaves have silver margins. The best color develops in the shade.

Alternate Species

A. genevensis (Geneva Bugleweed) is an upright, non-invasive species that grows 6–12" tall and 18" in spread. The spring flowers are blue, white or pink. Because this species is less invasive than *A. reptans*, it is more suitable in a rock garden or near a lawn.

Problems & Pests

Occasional problems with crown rot, leaf spot and root rot can be avoided by providing good air circulation and by making sure the plant is not standing in water for extended periods.

A. reptans (this page)

According to European folk myths, ajugas cause fires if brought into the house.

Anemone
Windflower

Anemone

Height: 3"–5' **Spread:** 6–24" **Flower color:** white, yellow, pink, blue, purple
Blooms: spring, summer, fall **Zones:** 5–8

ANYONE WHO HAS EVER SEEN a mature Japanese Anemone in full bloom will agree it takes center stage in late summer and early fall, when many other bloomers have faded. So why isn't this fabulous flowering machine as common as dust in perennial gardens? 'Tis a puzzle. Anemones have long taproots that take time to establish, so cut them some slack for the first couple of years. After that, stand back and enjoy the show.

Planting
Seeding: Not recommended
Planting out: Spring
Spacing: 4–18"

Growing

Anemones prefer **partial or light shade** but tolerate full sun. The soil should be of **average to high fertility, humus rich** and **moist**. Grecian Windflower prefers a light, sandy soil. While dormant, anemones should have dry soil. Mulch Japanese Anemone the first winter to help it establish.

Divide Grecian Windflower in summer and other anemones in spring or fall.

Deadhead only to keep a tidy look because removing spent flowers will not extend the bloom.

Tips

Anemones make a beautiful addition to lightly shaded borders, woodland gardens and rock gardens.

A. x *hybrida* (this page)

A. x hybrida (above),
A. blanda 'White Splendor' (below)

The name anemone (a-nem-o-nee) comes from the Greek anemos, 'wind,' referring to the windswept mountainside habitat of some species.

Recommended

A. blanda (Grecian Windflower) is a low, spreading, tuberous species that bears blue flowers in spring. It grows 6–8" tall, with an equal spread. **'Pink Star'** has pink flowers with yellow centers. **'White Splendor'** is a vigorous plant with white flowers.

A. canadensis (Meadow Anemone) is a spreading plant with slightly invasive tendencies. It grows 12–24" tall, with an equal spread. The white flowers with yellow centers are borne in late spring and early summer. This plant needs regular watering when first planted in order to become established.

A. x *hybrida* (Japanese Anemone) is an upright, suckering hybrid. It grows 2–5' tall, spreads about 24" and bears pink or white flowers from late summer to early fall. Many cultivars are commonly available.

'**Honorine Jobert**' has plentiful white flowers. '**Max Vogel**' has large pink flowers. '**Pamina**' has pinkish red double flowers. '**Whirlwind**' has white semi-double flowers.

A. nemerosa (Wood Anemone) is a low, creeping perennial that grows 3–10" tall and spreads 12" or more. The spring flowers are white, often flushed with pink. '**Flore Pleno**' has double white flowers. '**Rosea**' has red-purple flowers.

Problems & Pests

Rare but possible problems include leaf gall, downy mildew, smut, fungal leaf spot, powdery mildew, rust, nematodes, caterpillars, slugs and flea beetles.

A. x *hybrida* (this page)

Artemisia
Dusty Miller, Wormwood, Sage
Artemisia

Height: 6"–6' **Spread:** 12–36" **Flower color:** white or yellow, generally inconspicuous; plant grown for foliage **Blooms:** late summer, mid-fall **Zones:** 3–8

THE SILVER GRAY FOLIAGE of artemisias adds cool elegance to the perennial border and makes magic when companion plants are between blooms.
So in spite of their invasive habit, which has tarnished their reputation,
they remain a favorite of mine. Because artemisias are grown for their
foliage, which declines after blooming, they should not be allowed to flower.
Early pruning—cutting back by one-half in late May or early June—will
encourage compact, tidy growth and prevent flopping. 'Powis Castle' and
'Silver Brocade' demand superb drainage and do best in sandy soils. My
'Powis Castle' has thrived on neglect for five years planted in a one-gallon
container sunk in the clay soil of my garden.

Planting

Seeding: Not recommended

Planting out: Spring,
summer or fall

Spacing: 10–36"

Growing

Artemisias grow best in **full sun**. The soil should be of **average to high fertility** and **well drained**. These plants dislike wet, humid conditions.

Artemisias respond well to pruning in late spring. If you prune before May, frost may kill any new growth. Whenever artemisias begin to look straggly, they may be cut back hard to encourage new growth and maintain a neater form. Divide them every one or two years when plants appear to be thinning in the centers.

Tips

Artemisias can be used in rock gardens and borders. Their silver gray foliage makes them good backdrop plants behind brightly colored flowers, and they are useful for filling in spaces between other plants. Smaller forms may also be used to create knot gardens.

Some species can become invasive. If you want to control horizontal spreading of an artemisia, plant it in a bottomless container. Sunk into the ground, the container is hidden and it prevents the plant from spreading beyond the container's edges. You can maintain good drainage by removing the bottom of the container.

Recommended

A. absinthium (Common Wormwood) is a clump-forming, woody-based plant. It has aromatic, hairy, gray foliage and bears inconspicuous yellow flowers in late summer. It grows 24–36" tall

A. ludoviciana cultivar (above),
A. schmidtiana 'Nana' (below)

The genus name may honor either Artemisia, a botanist and medical researcher from around 350 BC, or Artemis, Goddess of the Hunt and the Moon in Greek mythology.

A. *ludoviciana* 'Valerie Finnis' (above), A. *ludoviciana* (below)

There are almost 300 species of Artemisia *distributed around the world.*

and spreads about 24". **'Lambrook Silver'** has attractive silver gray foliage. (Zones 4–8)

A. lactiflora (White Mugwort) is an upright, clump-forming species 4–6' tall and 24–36" in spread. This is one of the few artemisias to bear showy flowers; its attractive creamy white blooms appear from late summer to mid-fall. The foliage of this hardy species is dark green or gray-green.

A. ludoviciana (White Sage, Silver Sage) is an upright, clump-forming species. It grows 2–4' tall and spreads 24". The foliage is silvery white and the flowers are inconspicuous. The species is not grown as often as the cultivars. **'Silver Frost'** has narrow leaves that give the plant a soft, feathery appearance. It grows 18–24" tall, with an equal spread. **'Valerie Finnis'** is a good choice for hot, dry areas. It has very wide, silvery leaves, is less invasive than the species and combines beautifully with many other perennials. (Zones 4–8)

A. **'Powis Castle'** is compact, mounding and shrubby. It grows 24–36" tall, with an equal spread. It has feathery, silver gray foliage and inconspicuous flowers. This cultivar is reliably hardy to Zone 6, but with winter protection in a sheltered site it is worth trying in colder regions.

A. schmidtiana (Silvermound) is a low, dense, mound-forming perennial. It grows 12–24" tall and spreads 12–18". The foliage is feathery, hairy and silvery gray. **'Nana'** (Dwarf Silvermound) is very compact and grows only half the size of the species. This cultivar is extremely hardy and can be grown in all parts of Michigan.

A. stelleriana **'Silver Brocade'** is a low, somewhat spreading cultivar about 6" tall and up to 18" in spread. Its soft, pale gray leaves have rounded lobes. This very hardy cultivar can be grown all over Michigan.

Problems & Pests

Rust, downy mildew and other fungal diseases are possible problems for artemisias.

A. lactiflora (above),
A. ludoviciana cultivar (below)

Aster

Aster

Height: 1–5' **Spread:** 18–36" **Flower color:** red, white, blue, purple, pink
Blooms: late summer to mid-fall **Zones:** 3–8

ASTERS ARE A MIRACLE CURE for the late-summer flowering blues, and the hot pink 'Alma Potschke' stands at the top of my list. This well-behaved but flashy lady needs no staking or pinching to keep her under control. Pinching back New England Aster by half early in the season encourages side shoots and keep the plant from flopping. After asters' blooms have faded, prompt deadheading prevents these prolific producers from re-seeding. Combine tall asters with Boltonia, Japanese Anemone or goldenrods for a striking late-season display. Shorter varieties, such as 'Purple Dome,' cuddle up nicely to lady's mantles and lamb's ears.

Planting

Seeding: Not recommended
Planting out: Spring or fall
Spacing: 18–36"

Growing

Asters prefer **full sun** but tolerate partial shade. The soil should be **fertile, moist** and **well drained**. Pinch or shear these plants back in early summer to promote dense growth and reduce disease problems. Mulch in winter to protect plants from temperature fluctuations. Divide every two to three years to maintain vigor and control spread.

A. novi-belgii (this page)

Tips

Asters can be used in the middle of borders and in cottage gardens. These plants can also be naturalized in wild gardens.

These old-fashioned flowers were once called starworts because of the many petals that radiate out from the center of the flowerhead.

Recommended

A. x *frikartii* produces abundant and continuous blooms in light to dark shades of purple. These hybrids can be temperamental and may need re-planting after several years. They grow up to 24" tall and spread to 18". '**Mönch**' is a taller variety, up to 30", with abundant lavender blue flowers. (Zone 5 with protection)

A. *novae-angliae* (Michaelmas Daisy, New England Aster) is an upright, spreading, clump-forming

A. novi-belgii (above), *A. novae-angliae* (below)

perennial that grows to 5' tall and spreads to 24". It bears yellow-centered purple flowers. 'Alma Potschke' bears bright hot pink or cherry red flowers. It grows 3–4' tall and spreads 24". 'Purple Dome' is dwarf and spreading with dark purple flowers. It grows 18–24" tall and spreads 24–30". This cultivar resists mildew.

A. novi-belgii (Michaelmas Daisy, New York Aster) is a dense, upright, clump-forming perennial. It grows 3–4' tall and spreads 18–36". 'Alice Haslam' is a dwarf plant with bright pink flowers. It grows 10–18" tall and spreads 18". 'Chequers' is a compact plant with purple flowers.

Problems & Pests

Powdery mildew, aster wilt, aster yellows, aphids, mites, slugs and nematodes can cause trouble.

A. novi-belgii (this page)

What looks like a single flower of an aster, or of other daisy like plants, is actually a cluster of many tiny flowers. Look closely at the center of the flowerhead and you will see all the individual flowers.

Astilbe
Astilbe

Height: 1–4' **Spread:** 8–36" **Flower color:** white, pink, peach, purple, red
Blooms: late spring, summer **Zones:** 3–9

IF YOU'RE SEARCHING FOR TREASURE to add color to a summer shade garden, an astilbe (a-*stil*-bee) may be your pot of gold. Nest one in humus-rich soil that doesn't dry out, and you'll be rewarded with eye-catching, colorful plumes of flowers. Astilbes come in a wide range of heights, colors and bloom times, so plant a mix of cultivars to extend flowering. A meal of slow-release fertilizer in spring helps keep these heavy feeders happy.

Planting

Seeding: Not recommended; seedlings do not come true to type

Planting out: Spring

Spacing: 18–36"

Growing

Astilbes enjoy **light or partial shade** and tolerate full shade, though with reduced flowering in deep shade. The soil should be **fertile, humus rich, acidic, moist** and **well drained.** Astilbes like to grow near water sources, such as ponds and streams, but they dislike standing in water. Provide a mulch in summer to keep the roots cool and moist. Divide every three years in spring or fall to maintain plant vigor.

Tips

Astilbes can be grown near the edges of bog gardens or ponds and in woodland gardens and shaded borders.

The root crown of an astilbe tends to lift out of the soil as the plant grows bigger. This problem can be solved by applying a top dressing of rich soil as a mulch when the plant starts lifting or by lifting the entire plant and re-planting it deeper into the soil.

In late summer, transplant seedlings found near the parent plant for plumes of color throughout the garden.

A. japonica 'Deutschland'

Astilbe flowers fade to various shades of brown. Deadheading will not extend the bloom, so the choice is yours whether to remove the spent blossoms. Astilbes self-seed easily and the flowerheads look interesting and natural in the garden well into fall. Self-seeded plants are unlikely to look like the parent plant.

Recommended

A. x *arendsii* (Astilbe, False Spirea) grows 18"–4' tall and spreads 18–36". Many cultivars are available from this hybrid group, including the following popular selections. **'Avalanche'** bears white flowers in late summer. **'Bressingham Beauty'** bears bright pink flowers in mid-summer. **'Cattleya'** bears reddish pink flowers in mid-summer. **'Fanal'** bears red flowers in early summer and features deep bronze foliage.

A. x *arendsii* (this page)

'Weisse Gloria' bears creamy white flowers in mid- to late summer.

A. chinensis (Chinese Astilbe) is a dense, vigorous perennial that tolerates dry soil better than other astilbe species. It grows about 24" tall and spreads 18". It bears fluffy white, pink or purple flowers in late summer. **Var.** *pumila* is more commonly found than the species. This plant forms a low groundcover 10" tall and 8" in spread. It bears dark pink flowers. **'Superba'** is a tall form with lavender purple flowers produced in a long narrow spike.

A. japonica (Japanese Astilbe) is a compact, clump-forming perennial. The species is rarely grown in favor of the cultivars. **'Deutschland'** grows 20" in height and spreads 12".

It bears white flowers in late spring. **'Etna'** grows 24–30" tall and spreads 18–24". It bears dark red flowers in early summer. **'Peach Blossom'** bears peach pink flowers in early summer. It grows about 20" tall.

Problems & Pests

A variety of pests, such as whiteflies, black vine weevils and Japanese beetles, can occasionally attack astilbes. Powdery mildew, bacterial leaf spot and fungal leaf spot are also possible problems.

Astilbes make great cut flowers, and if you leave the plumes in a vase as the water evaporates, you'll have dried flowers to enjoy all winter.

A. x arendsii

Basket-of-Gold
Aurinia

Height: 6–12" **Spread:** 8–18" **Flower color:** yellow, occasionally apricot
Blooms: mid-spring **Zones:** 3–7

THIS GLOWING GOLD HARBINGER of spring makes a nice foil for colorful tulips. Its beauty fades in summer, though, so place it at a distance or combine it with taller companion plants to help mask tatty foliage. Keep it away from less vigorous plants, because Basket-of-Gold likes to spread. A patio, walkway or driveway will help contain excessive growth.

Planting

Seeding: Sow seeds in containers in cold frame in spring

Planting out: Early to mid-spring

Spacing: 12–18"

Growing

Basket-of-gold prefers **full sun.** The soil should be of **average to poor fertility, sandy** and **well drained.** Amend clay soils with gravel and organic matter to improve the drainage. Basket-of-gold may rot in wet soil, and growth becomes floppy in rich soil. It is drought tolerant. Established plants should not be moved or divided.

Shear Basket-of-gold back lightly after flowering to keep the plant compact and perhaps encourage a few more flowers. Do not shear off all flowerheads in hot regions, because the plants will not

live as long when exposed to high temperatures. Self-seeding provides new plants as the old ones die out. Cuttings can be taken from the new growth that emerges after flowering.

Tips

Use this plant in borders and rock gardens, along wall tops and as a groundcover in difficult or little-used areas. Avoid planting Basket-of-gold near slow-growing plants because it can quickly choke them out.

Recommended

A. saxatilis is a vigorous, mound-forming perennial with bright yellow flowers. It grows 8–12" tall and spreads 12–18" or more. '**Citrina**' bears light lemon yellow flowers. '**Compacta**' bears golden yellow flowers. It is a bit smaller than the

species, growing about 6" tall and spreading 8". **'Dudley Nevill'** bears apricot-colored flowers. **'Gold Ball'** is a clump-forming plant with bright yellow flowers held above the foliage. **'Variegata'** bears lemon yellow flowers and has irregular cream-colored margins on the foliage.

Problems & Pests

Basket-of-gold generally has no serious problems but can rot in wet soil.

Basket-of-gold belongs to the mustard family, which includes such plants as cabbage and broccoli.

Bellflower
Campanula

Height: 4"–6' **Spread:** 12–36" **Flower color:** blue, white, purple
Blooms: summer, early fall **Zones:** 3–7

THIS HUGE AND COLORFUL GROUP OF PERENNIALS, comprising dozens of species, cultivars and varieties, includes a wide range of growth habits, from 4' showstoppers to dainty 6" lovelies. And if blue, lavender and purple are your colors, you may want to become a bellflower collector, for there is a plant to suit almost any part of the garden. The low-growing, large-flowered Carpathian Bellflower mixed with sedum and lady's mantle makes a delightful edging for borders and walkways. For many gardens, the belle of the ball in the summer-flowering border may be the taller Peach-leaved Bellflower. Shasta Daisy, yarrows and Garden Phlox all make lovely companions.

Planting

Seeding: Not recommended because germination can be erratic, but if done, direct sow in spring or fall

Planting out: Spring or fall

Spacing: 12–36"

Bellflowers can be propagated by basal, new-growth or rhizome cuttings.

Growing

Bellflowers grow well in **full sun, partial shade** or **light shade**. The soil should be of **average to high fertility** and **well drained**. Bellflowers appreciate a mulch to keep their roots cool and moist in summer and protected in winter, particularly if snow cover is inconsistent. It is important to divide bellflowers every few years in early spring or late summer to keep plants vigorous and to prevent them from becoming invasive.

Deadhead to prolong blooming. Use scissors to cut back one-third of the plant at a time, allowing other sections to continue blooming. As the pruned section starts to bud, cut back other sections for continued blooming.

Tips

Low, spreading and trailing bellflowers can be used in rock gardens and on rock walls. Upright and mounding bellflowers can be used in borders and cottage gardens. You can also edge beds with the low-growing varieties.

C. persicifolia (above),
C. carpatica (below)

Deadheading promptly by removing individual spent flowers will keep bellflowers looking tidy and will extend their bloom time.

C. poscharskyana

Recommended

C. **'Birch Hybrid'** is low growing and spreading. It bears light blue to mauve flowers in summer.

C. carpatica (Carpathian Bellflower, Carpathian Harebell) is a spreading, mounding perennial. It grows 10–12" tall, spreads 12–24" and bears blue, white or purple flowers in summer. **'Blue Clips'** is a smaller, compact plant with large blue flowers. **'Bressingham White'** is a compact plant with large white flowers. **'Jewel'** is low growing with deep blue flowers. It grows 4–8" tall. **'Kent Belle'** is a stately new hybrid with large, deep violet blue bells on arching stems.

C. glomerata (Clustered Bellflower) forms a clump of upright stems. It grows 12–24" tall, with an equal or greater spread. Clusters of purple, blue or white flowers are borne over most of the summer. **'Superba'** has dark purple flowers.

C. lactiflora (Milky Bellflower) is an upright perennial 4–6' tall and about 24" in spread. It bears white, light to dark blue, or light to dark

purple flowers in summer. **Var.** *alba* ('Alba') bears white flowers.

C. persicifolia (Peach-leaved Bellflower) is an upright perennial. It grows about 36" tall and spreads about 12". It bears white, blue or purple flowers from early summer to mid-summer.

C. portenschlagiana (Dalmation Bellflower) is a low, spreading, mounding perennial. It grows 6" tall and spreads 20–24". It bears light or deep purple flowers from mid- to late summer.

C. poscharskyana (Serbian Bellflower) is a trailing perennial. It grows 6–12" tall and spreads 24–36". It bears light purple flowers in summer and early fall.

Problems & Pests

Minor problems with vine weevils, spider mites, aphids, slugs, powdery mildew, rust and fungal leaf spot are possible.

C. carpatica

Over 300 species of Campanula *grow throughout the Northern Hemisphere in habitats ranging from high, rocky crags to boggy meadows.*

Bergamot
Bee Balm
Monarda

Height: 2–4' **Spread:** 12–24" **Flower color:** red, pink, purple
Blooms: late summer **Zones:** 3–9

FOR AN OUTSTANDING DISPLAY OF COLOR, it's hard to beat *Monarda*. Plant it and hummingbirds, butterflies and curious observers will flock to your garden to see what's blooming. The intensely red 'Gardenview Scarlet' and vibrant pink 'Marshall's Delight' are disease-resistant favorites. Almost any of the summer-flowering perennials make good companion plants, including yarrows, Balloon Flower and *Salvia* 'May Night.'

Planting

Seeding: Start seeds outdoors in cold frame or indoors in early spring

Planting out: Spring or fall

Spacing: 18–24"

Growing

Bergamot grows well in **full sun, partial shade** or **light shade**. The soil should be of **average fertility, humus rich, moist** and **well drained**. Dry conditions encourage mildew and loss of leaves, so regular watering is a must. Divide every two or three years in spring just as new growth emerges.

Cut back some of the stems by half in May to extend the flowering period and encourage compact growth. Thinning the stems in spring also helps prevent powdery mildew. If mildew strikes after flowering, cut the plants back to 6" to increase air circulation.

The genus name honors Spanish botanist and physician Nicholas Monardes (1493–1588).

'Marshall's Delight'

Tips

Use Bergamot beside a stream or pond, or in a lightly shaded, well-watered border.

The fresh or dried leaves may be used to make a refreshing, minty, citrus-scented tea. Put a handful of fresh leaves in a teapot, pour boiling water over them and let steep for at least five minutes. Sweeten the tea with honey to taste.

Bergamot attract bees, butterflies and hummingbirds to your garden. Avoid using pesticides, which can seriously harm or kill these creatures and which will prevent you from using the plant for culinary or medicinal purposes.

Recommended

M. didyma is a bushy, mounding plant that forms a thick clump of stems with red, pink or purple flowers. '**Gardenview Scarlet**' bears large scarlet flowers and resists powdery mildew. '**Marshall's Delight**' doesn't come true to type from seed and

must be propagated by cuttings or divisions. It is very resistant to powdery mildew and bears pink flowers. **'Panorama'** is a group of hybrids with flowers in scarlet, pink, purple or salmon.

Problems & Pests

Powdery mildew is the worst problem, but rust, leaf spot and leafhoppers can cause trouble. Don't allow the plant to dry out for extended periods.

The common name, Bergamot, comes from the scent of the Italian Bergamot orange (Citrus bergamia) *often used in aromatherapy.*

Bergenia

Bergenia

Height: 12–24" **Spread:** 12–24" or more **Flower color:** red, purple, light to dark pink, white **Blooms:** spring **Zones:** 3–8

THE SPRING-FLOWERING BERGENIAS are grown for their foliage as well as their blossoms. Their cabbage-like leaves form in large rosettes and turn burgundy in fall. These deer-resistant plants look best when planted in groups. For the most vigorous growth, place them in a shaded area that receives morning sun. Purple Bergenia's deep purple leaves suffer less damage over the winter than most.

Planting

Seeding: Seeds may not come true to type. Fresh, ripe seeds should be sown uncovered, either indoors or in the garden. Keep soil temperature at 69–70° F.

Planting out: Spring

Spacing: 10–20"

Growing

Bergenias grow well in **full sun** or **partial shade.** The soil should be of **average to rich fertility** and **well drained.** A **moist** soil is preferable, especially when plants are grown in full sun, but these plants are somewhat drought tolerant once established. Divide every two to three years when the clump begins to die out in the middle.

Propagating by seed can be somewhat risky; you may not get what you hoped for. A more certain way to get more of the plants you have is to propagate them with root cuttings. Bergenias spread just below the surface by rhizomes, which may be cut off in pieces and grown separately as long as

B. cordifolia (below)

a leaf shoot is attached to the section. Top-dress soil with compost in spring if rhizomes appear to be lifting out of the soil.

Tips

These versatile, low-growing, spreading plants can be used as groundcovers, as edging along borders and pathways, as part of rock gardens and in mass plantings under trees and shrubs.

Once flowering is complete, in early spring, bergenias still make a beautiful addition to the garden with their thick, leathery, glossy leaves. A bergenia provides a soothing background for other flowers with its expanse of green. As well, many varieties turn attractive shades of bronze and purple in fall and winter.

Recommended

B. 'Bressingham White' grows about 12" tall and has white flowers.

B. ciliata (Winter Bergenia) grows 18–24" tall, with an equal spread. Its flowers are white or light pink.

B. cordifolia (Heart-leaved Bergenia) grows about 24" tall, with an equal or greater spread. Its flowers

These plants are also called elephant ears, because of the large leathery leaves, and pigsqueak, for the unusual sound made when a leaf is rubbed briskly between thumb and forefinger.

B. cordifolia

are deep pink, and the foliage turns bronze or purple in fall and winter. '**Purpurea**' has magenta purple flowers and red-tinged foliage.

B. '**Evening Glow**' ('Abdënglut') grows about 12" tall and spreads 18–24". The flowers are a deep magenta-crimson. The foliage turns red and maroon in the winter.

B. purpurascens (Purple Bergenia) grows about 18" tall and spreads about 12". The young leaves are red, as are the undersides of mature leaves. In winter the entire leaves turn purple or red again. Deep purple flowers are borne in mid- or late spring.

B. x *schmidtii* is a compact plant that grows 12" tall and spreads 24". The flowers are pink.

B. '**Winter Fairy Tale**' ('Wintermärchen') grows 12–18" tall and spreads 18–24". The flowers are rose red, and the dark green leaves are touched with red in winter.

Problems & Pests
Rare problems with fungal leaf spot, root rot, weevils, slugs, caterpillars and foliar nematodes are possible.

Black-Eyed Susan
Rudbeckia

Height: 18"–10' **Spread:** 12–36" **Flower color:** yellow or orange, with brown or green centers **Blooms:** mid-summer to fall **Zones:** 3–9

BLACK-EYED SUSANS HAVE BECOME MAINSTAYS in Michigan landscapes, and with good reason. They are tough as nails, and 'Goldsturm,' named a Plant of the Year by the American Perennial Plant Association, leads the pack. It bears plentiful yellow, daisy-like flowers with dark brown centers from mid-summer until the first hard frost. Gardeners with room to spare should give the drooping-petaled, greenish-centered 'Herbstsonne' a try—it can climb to heights of 7'. Cut it back by half when it reaches 2' to keep it in the more manageable 5' range.

Planting

Seeding: Start seed in a cold frame or indoors in early spring. Soil temperature should be about 61–64° F.

Planting out: Spring

Spacing: 12–36"

Black-eyed Susan cut flowers are long lasting in arrangements.

Growing

Black-eyed Susans grow well in **full sun** or **partial shade**. The soil should be of **average fertility** and **well drained**. Fairly heavy clay soils are tolerated. Regular watering is best, but established plants are drought tolerant. Divide in spring or fall every three to five years.

Pinch plants in June to make shorter, bushier stands.

Tips

Use black-eyed Susans in wildflower or naturalistic gardens, in borders and in cottage-style gardens. They are best planted in masses and drifts.

Though deadheading early in the season keeps the plants flowering vigorously, seedheads are often left in place later in the season for winter interest and as food for birds in fall and winter.

Recommended

R. fulgida is an upright, spreading plant. It grows 18–36" tall and spreads 12–24". The orange-yellow flowers have brown centers.

R. fulgida

Var. *sullivantii* '**Goldsturm**' bears large, bright golden yellow flowers.

R. laciniata (Cutleaf Coneflower) forms a large, open clump. It grows 4–10' tall and spreads 24–36". The yellow flowers have green centers. The cultivar '**Goldquelle**' grows 36" tall and has bright yellow double flowers.

R. nitida is an upright, spreading plant 3–6' tall and 24–36" wide. The yellow flowers have green centers. '**Autumn Glory**' has golden yellow flowers. '**Herbstsonne**' ('Autumn Sun') has bright golden yellow flowers.

Problems & Pests

Rare problems with slugs, aphids, rust, smut and leaf spot are possible.

R. fulgida with *Echinacea*

Blanket Flower
Gaillardia

Height: 12–36" **Spread:** 12–24" **Flower color:** combinations of red and yellow **Blooms:** early summer to early fall **Zones:** 3–10

THIS OLD-FASHIONED PRAIRIE NATIVE is coming back into style as gardeners strive to find easy-care plants that can take a licking. This drought-, heat- and salt-tolerant dynamo is great for hot, dry beds that bank pavement. Occasional deadheading will help keep the blooms coming. Heavy, wet soils in winter spell the demise of Blanket Flower, so a raised bed or a berm makes a good home for this colorful character.

Planting

Seeding: Start seed indoors or in the garden in early spring; don't cover the seeds because they need light to germinate

Planting out: Spring

Spacing: 18"

The multi-colored petals of Gaillardia *(gay-lard-ee-a) flowers add a fiery glow to cottage gardens and meadow plantings.*

Growing

Blanket Flower grows best in **full sun**. The soil should be **fertile, light** and **well drained**. Poor soils are tolerated, but plants will not overwinter in heavy, wet soil. Deadheading encourages the plants to bloom all summer. Cut the plants back to within 6" of the ground in late summer to encourage new growth and promote the longevity of these often short-lived plants.

Tips

Blanket Flower is a North American prairie plant that looks at home in an informal cottage garden, wildflower garden or meadow planting. It is also attractive when planted in clumps of three or four in a mixed or herbaceous border. Drought tolerant, it is ideal for neglected and rarely watered parts of the garden. Dwarf varieties make good container plantings.

Recommended

G. x grandiflora is a bushy, upright plant 24–36" tall and 12–24" in spread. It bears daisy-like flowers all summer and into early fall. The petals have yellow tips and red bases. **'Burgundy'** is 24–36" tall and has dark red blooms. **'Dwarf Goblin'** ('Kobold') is a compact cultivar that grows only 12" tall. The flowers are variegated red and yellow, like those of the species.

Problems & Pests

Powdery mildew, downy mildew, leaf spot, rust, aster yellows and leafhoppers are possible, but rarely cause much trouble.

Almost all Gaillardia *species are native to the United States, usually found growing wild on the prairies.*

G. x grandiflora with Echinops

Blazing Star
Spike Gayfeather, Gayfeather
Liatris

Height: 18–36" **Spread:** 18–24" **Flower color:** purple, white
Blooms: summer **Zones:** 3–9

THIS HARDY MICHIGAN NATIVE, with its colorful, fuzzy, spiked blooms, makes a dynamic vertical accent in the summer garden. You can encourage re-blooming by cutting the entire spike back to the basal foliage when two-thirds of the flowering is complete. Group Blazing Star with Purple Cone-flower, phloxes and Perovskia, and skirt it with 'Moonbeam' coreopsis. Hummingbirds and butterflies love this plant, so place it where you can sit and enjoy the show.

Planting

Seeding: Direct sow in fall. Plants may take two to four years to bloom from seed.

Planting out: Spring

Spacing: 18–24"

The spikes make excellent, long-lasting cut flowers.

Growing

Blazing Star prefers **full sun**. The soil should be of **average fertility, sandy** and **humus rich**. Water well during the growing season, but don't allow the plants to stand in water during cool weather. Mulch during summer to prevent moisture loss. Divide every three or four years in fall. The clump will appear crowded when it is time to divide.

Trim off the spent flower spikes to promote a longer blooming period and to keep Blazing Star looking tidy.

Tips

Use this plant in borders and meadow plantings. Plant in a location that has good drainage to avoid root rot in winter. Blazing Star does well when grown in planters.

Recommended

L. spicata is an erect, clump-forming plant. The flowers are pinkish purple or white. **'Floristan Violet'** has purple flowers. **'Floristan White'** has white flowers. **'Kobold'** has deep purple flowers.

Problems & Pests

Slugs, stem rot, root rot, rust and leaf spot are possible problems.

'Kobold' (below)

Bleeding Heart
Dicentra

Height: 1–4' **Spread:** 1–3' **Flower color:** pink, white, red
Blooms: spring, summer **Zones:** 3–9

WITH THEIR DOZENS OF HEART-SHAPED LOCKETS dangling from gracefully arching stems, the delicate and delightful bleeding hearts, often dismissed as woodland plants, adapt to most gardens. These plants do well in sunny spaces but enjoy a respite of afternoon shade and a blanket of fluffy mulch to keep the soil cool and moist. Common Bleeding Heart goes dormant when the weather heats up, but Fringed Bleeding Heart keeps its delicate foliage and provides sporadic bloom throughout the summer if kept deadheaded. In a shaded setting the bleeding hearts pair nicely with ferns, hostas or pulmonarias.

Planting

Seeding: Start freshly ripened seed in a cold frame. Plants self-seed in the garden.

Planting out: Spring

Spacing: 18–36"

Growing

Bleeding hearts prefer **light shade** but tolerate partial shade or full shade. The soil should be **humus rich, moist** and **well drained**. Though these plants prefer to remain evenly moist, they tolerate drought quite well, particularly if the weather doesn't get hot. Very dry summer conditions cause the plants to die back, but they revive in fall or the following spring. It is most important for bleeding hearts to remain moist while blooming in order to prolong the flowering period. Constant summer moisture will keep the flowers coming until mid-summer.

Common Bleeding Heart and Fringed Bleeding Heart rarely need dividing. Divide Western Bleeding Heart every three years or so.

D. formosa (this page)

These delicate plants are the perfect addition to a moist woodland garden. Plant them next to a shaded pond or stream.

Tips

Bleeding hearts can be naturalized in a woodland garden or grown in a border or rock garden. They make excellent early-season specimen plants. They also do well near a pond or stream.

Recommended

D. 'Adrian Bloom' forms a compact clump of dark gray-green foliage. It grows about 12" tall and spreads about 18". Bright red flowers are produced in late spring and continue to appear intermittently all summer.

D. exima (Fringed Bleeding Heart) forms a loose mounded clump of lacy, fern-like foliage. It grows 15–24" tall and spreads about 18". The pink or white flowers are borne mostly in spring, but may be produced sporadically over summer. Unless kept well watered, the plant will go dormant during hot, dry weather in summer.

D. formosa (Western Bleeding Heart) is a low-growing, wide-spreading plant. It grows about 18" tall and spreads 24–36". The pink flowers fade to white as they mature. This plant is likely to self-seed. It is the most drought tolerant of the bleeding hearts and is the most likely to continue

D. spectabilis (above),
D. s. 'Alba' (below)

flowering all summer. It can become invasive.
Var. *alba* has white flowers.

D. **'Luxuriant'** is a low-growing hybrid with blue-green foliage and red-pink flowers. It grows about 12" tall and spreads about 18". Flowers appear in spring and early summer.

D. spectabilis (Common Bleeding Heart) forms a large, elegant mound up to 4' tall and about 18" in spread. It blooms in late spring and early summer. The inner petals are white and the outer petals are pink. This species is likely to die back in the summer heat and prefers light dappled shade. **'Alba'** has entirely white flowers.

D. **'Stuart Boothman'** is a spreading perennial with blue-gray foliage. It grows about 12" tall, with an equal or greater spread. Dark pink flowers are produced over a long period from spring to mid-summer.

Problems & Pests

Slugs, downy mildew, *Verticillium* wilt, viruses, rust and fungal leaf spot can cause occasional problems.

D. exima (this page)

Boltonia
Boltonia

Height: 3–6' **Spread:** up to 4' **Flower color:** white, mauve or pink, with yellow centers **Blooms:** late summer and fall **Zones:** 4–9

IF THE CASUAL LOOK OF A COTTAGE GARDEN pleases you and there is good space at the back of the border, fill it with Boltonia. The large clouds of dainty, daisy-like flowers will billow from September to frost. Good companions include 'Chocolate' Joe-Pye weed, 'Autumn Joy' sedum, Perovskia and caryopteris, along with any of the fall-blooming asters. Boltonia is a Michigan native, and seed collected from the species is easy to grow. Seed collected from 'Snowbank,' however, will not come true.

Planting

Seeding: Start seed in a cold frame in fall

Planting out: Spring or fall

Spacing: 36"

Growing

Boltonia prefers **full sun** but tolerates partial shade. It prefers soil that is **fertile, humus rich, moist** and **well drained** but adapts to less fertile soils and tolerates some drought. Divide in fall or early spring when the clump is becoming overgrown or seems to be dying out in the middle.

Staking may be required, particularly in somewhat shaded sites. Use twiggy branches or a peony hoop to provide support. If installed while the plant is young, the stakes will be hidden by the growing branches.

Tips

This large plant can be used in the middle or at the back of a mixed border, in a naturalized or cottage-style garden or near a pond or other water feature.

A good alternative to Michaelmas Daisy, Boltonia is less susceptible to powdery mildew.

Recommended

B. asteroides is a large, upright perennial with narrow, grayish green leaves. It bears lots of white or slightly purple daisy-like flowers with yellow centers. **'Pink Beauty'** has a looser habit and bears pale pink flowers. **'Snowbank'** has a denser, more compact habit and bears more plentiful white flowers than the species.

Problems & Pests

Boltonia has rare problems with rust, leaf spot and powdery mildew.

Boltonia is native to the eastern and central United States.

Brunnera
Siberian Bugloss
Brunnera

Height: 12–18" **Spread:** 18–24" **Flower color:** blue
Blooms: spring **Zones:** 3–8

SOMETIMES IT TAKES A NEW INTRODUCTION, such as the lovely variegated Brunnera, to focus a gardener's attention on a really useful plant. And such is the case with this lovely woodland dweller. Often mistaken for forget-me-not blooms, the tiny blue flowers burst forth in spring, followed by mounds of large, heart-shaped leaves. Under the right conditions, flowering continues into early summer. The variegated varieties 'Hadspen Cream' and 'Dawson's White' feature foliage with luscious combinations of cream and green and will star in any cool, moist shade garden.

This reliable plant rarely suffers from any problems.

Planting

Seeding: Start seeds in a cold frame in early fall or indoors in early spring

Planting out: Spring

Spacing: 12–18"

Growing

Brunnera prefers **light shade** but tolerates morning sun when it has consistent moisture. The soil should be of **average fertility, humus rich, moist** and **well drained**. The species and its cultivars do not tolerate drought. Divide in spring when the center of the clump appears to be dying out.

Cut back faded foliage mid-season to produce a flush of new growth.

Tips

Brunnera makes a great addition to a woodland or shaded garden. Its low, bushy habit makes it useful as a groundcover or as an addition to a shaded border.

Recommended

B. macrophylla forms a mound of soft, heart-shaped leaves and produces loose clusters of blue flowers all spring. **'Dawson's White'** ('Variegata') has large leaves with irregular creamy patches. **'Hadspen Cream'** has leaves with creamy margins. Grow variegated plants in light or full shade to avoid scorched leaves.

Brunnera is related to borage and forget-me-nots.

Butterfly Weed
Asclepias

Height: 18–36" **Spread:** 12–24" **Flower color:** orange, yellow, white, red, pink, light purple **Blooms:** late spring, summer, early fall **Zones:** 4–9

A SHOWY, BRIGHT ORANGE BUTTERFLY MAGNET, *A. tuberosa* is native to the prairies, so it tolerates poor soil and drought. Following Mother Nature's lead, leave the plant intact over the winter so that the dried seedpods add interest to the garden, and cut it back in late spring. Pair this bright light with Little Bluestem, coreopsis and 'Victoria' salvia. *A. incarnata*, another Michigan native, has deep rose flowers and is a colorful choice for wet areas and bog gardens. 'Ice Ballet,' a charming white cultivar of this species, makes a nice addition to full-sun gardens with moist soil conditions.

Planting
Seeding: Start fresh seed in cold frame in early spring

Planting out: Spring

Spacing: 12–24"

Growing

Butterfly weeds prefer **full sun**. *A. tuberosa* grows in any **well-drained** soil but prefers a **fertile** soil. It is drought tolerant. *A. incarnata* prefers a **moist** or **boggy, fertile** soil.

To propagate, remove the plantlets that grow around the base of the plants. The deep taproot makes division very difficult.

Deadhead to encourage a second blooming.

Tips

Use *A. tuberosa* in meadow plantings and borders, on dry banks, in neglected areas and in wildflower, cottage and butterfly gardens. Use *A. incarnata* in moist borders and in bog, pondside or streamside plantings.

Butterfly weeds are slow to start in spring. Place a marker beside each plant in fall so you won't forget the plant is there and inadvertently dig it up.

Recommended

A. incarnata (Swamp Milkweed) grows about 36" tall and spreads up to 12". It bears clusters of pink, white or light purple flowers in late spring or early summer. Though it naturally grows in moist areas, it appreciates a well-drained soil in the garden. 'Ice Ballet' bears white flowers.

A. tuberosa forms a clump of upright, leafy stems. It grows 18–36" tall and spreads 12–24". It bears clusters of orange flowers in midsummer to early fall. 'Gay Butterflies' bears orange, yellow or red flowers.

Problems & Pests

Aphids and mealybugs can cause occasional problems.

A. tuberosa (above),
A. tuberosa with *Liatris* (below)

Native to North America, the butterfly weeds are a major food source for the Monarch butterfly and will attract butterflies to your garden.

Candytuft
Iberis

Height: 6–12" **Spread:** 10–36" **Flower color:** white **Blooms:** long period in spring; sometimes again in fall **Zones:** 3–9

'MY GRANDMOTHER GREW THIS IN HER GARDEN' is a phrase often heard when folks discover Candytuft blooming in garden centers. Plant it in areas protected from fierce weather, and this old-fashioned harbinger of spring will perk up the landscape with crisp white mounds of flowers. Fast-draining soils and a winter mulch of evergreen boughs are keys to success. For more flowers in fall, plant 'Autumn Snow,' the best of the repeat bloomers.

Planting

Seeding: Direct sow in spring

Planting out: Spring

Spacing: 6–12"

Growing

Candytuft prefers **full sun**. The soil should be of **poor to average fertility, moist, well drained** and **neutral to alkaline**.

In spring, cut away any brown sections when the new buds begin to break. As the stems spread, they may root where they touch the ground. These rooted ends may be cut away and re-planted elsewhere.

Candytuft should be sheared back by about one-third once it has finished flowering to promote new, compact growth. Every two or three years it should be sheared back by one-half to two-thirds to discourage the development of too much woody growth and to encourage abundant flowering. Division is rarely required.

Tips

Use Candytuft as an edging plant, in borders and rock gardens, in the crevices of rock walls and as a companion for spring-blooming bulbs.

Recommended

I. sempervirens is a spreading evergreen that grows 6–12" tall and spreads 16–36". It bears clusters of tiny white flowers. **'Autumn Snow'** bears white flowers in spring and fall. **'Little Gem'** is a compact, spring-flowering plant that spreads only 10". **'Snowflake'** ('Schneeflock') is a mounding plant that bears large white flowers in spring.

Problems & Pests

Occasional problems with slugs, caterpillars, damping off, gray mold, and fungal leaf spot are possible.

If you arrive home after dusk on a spring night, the white flowers of Candytuft will welcome you with a lovely glow in the moonlight.

Cardinal Flower
Lobelia
Lobelia

Height: 2–4' **Spread:** 12–24" **Flower color:** red, pink, white, blue, purple
Blooms: summer to fall **Zones:** 3–9

CARDINAL FLOWERS ARE TREASURED by full-sun and partial-shade gardeners who want to fend off the late-summer blahs in the garden. These treasures, though, can be tricky to winter over, so don't take it personally if they disappear by spring. Making sure the soil stays moist, leaving the stem intact over winter and providing a light mulch that is removed promptly in spring will help. In shady spots, these plants are outstanding when planted among ferns, hostas and assorted groundcovers. Hummingbirds and butterflies will love you for growing them.

Planting
Seeding: Sow in garden or cold frame in spring, when soil temperature is about 70° F

Planting out: Spring

Spacing: 12–18"

Growing

Cardinal flowers grow well in **full sun, light shade** and **partial shade**. The soil should be **fertile, slightly acidic** and **moist**. Never allow the soil to dry out for extended periods, especially in a sunny garden. Provide a mulch over winter to protect the plants. Divide every two to three years in fall to stimulate growth. To divide, lift the entire plant and remove the new rosettes growing at the plant base. Re-plant immediately in the garden.

Pinch plants in early summer to produce compact growth. Deadheading may encourage a second set of blooms.

Cardinal flowers self-seed quite easily. Because these plants are short lived, lasting about four or five years, self-seeding is an easy way to ensure continuing generations of plants. If you remove the spent flower spikes, be sure to allow at least a few of them to remain to spread their seeds. Don't worry too much, though—the lower flowers on a spike are likely to set seed before the top flowers are finished opening.

L. siphilitica (above),
L. cardinalis (below)

L. cardinalis (this page)

Tips

These plants are best used in streamside or pond-side plantings or in bog gardens.

Cardinal flowers may require a more acidic soil than other plants growing along a pondside. If this is the case, they may be planted in a container of peat-based potting soil and sunk into the ground at the edge of the pond.

Recommended

L. cardinalis (Cardinal Flower) forms an erect clump of bronzy green leaves. It grows 2–4' tall and spreads 12–24". It bears spikes of bright red

flowers from summer to fall. **'Alba'** has white blooms and is not as hardy as the species.

L. **'La Fresco'** bears jewel-toned, plum purple flowers.

L. **'Queen Victoria'** forms a clump of reddish stems with maroon foliage and scarlet flowers. It grows about 36" tall and spreads 12".

L. siphilitica (Great Blue Lobelia, Blue Cardinal Flower) forms an erect clump with bright green foliage. It grows 2–4' tall and spreads 12–18". Spikes of deep blue flowers are produced from mid-summer to fall. **Var.** *alba* has white flowers.

L. x *speciosa* (Hybrid Cardinal Flower) is the hardiest, most vigorous of the cardinal flowers. **'Complement'** has dark green foliage and bears red or blue-purple flowers.

L. **'Wildwood Splendor'** is a vigorous plant bearing deep purple flowers.

Problems & Pests

Rare problems with slugs, rust, smut and leaf spot can occur.

Lobelia was named after the Flemish botanist Mathias de l'Obel (1538–1616).

L. cardinalis cultivar (right),
L. 'Queen Victoria' (below)

Catmint
Nepeta

Height: 10–36" **Spread:** 18–36" **Flower color:** blue, purple, white, pink
Blooms: spring, summer, sometimes again in fall **Zones:** 3–8

THESE HARDY, DEER-RESISTANT members of the mint family make an
appealing, fuzzy, gray-green edging in herb gardens and other spaces where
a relaxed habit is appropriate. The taller, long-blooming 'Six Hills Giant,'
with its billowing lavender flowers, is a colorful choice for perennial gardens,
but without a mid-season haircut this character develops a messy cowlick.
Prompt deadheading or shearing as soon as the blooms begin to fade keeps
the foliage looking fresh and encourages re-blooming. 'Walker's Low' is a
dwarf variety that's good for rock gardens.

Planting

Seeding: Most popular hybrids and cultivars are sterile and cannot be grown from seed

Planting out: Spring

Spacing: 18–24"

Growing

Catmints grow well in **full sun** or **partial shade**. The soil should be of **average fertility** and **well drained**. The growth tends to be floppy in rich soil. Divide in spring or fall when the plants begin to look overgrown and dense.

Pinch tips in June to delay flowering and make the plants more compact. Once the plants are almost finished blooming, you may cut them back by one-third to one-half to encourage new growth and more blooms in late summer or fall.

Tips

Catmints can be used to edge borders and pathways. They work well in herb gardens and with roses in cottage gardens. Taller varieties make

Catmints have long been cultivated for their reputed medicinal and culinary qualities.

'Six Hills Giant'

lovely additions to perennial gardens, and dwarf types can be used in rock gardens.

Think twice before you grow *N. cataria* (Catnip) because cats are attracted to this plant. You may be laying out a welcome mat for the neighborhood cats to come and enjoy your garden. Cats do like the other catmints too, but not quite to the same extent.

Recommended

N. 'Blue Beauty' ('Souvenir d'André Chaudron') forms an upright, spreading clump. It grows 18–36" tall and spreads about 18". The gray-green foliage is fragrant and the large flowers are dark purple-blue.

N. x *faassenii* forms a clump of upright and spreading stems. It grows 18–36" tall, with an equal spread, and bears spikes of blue or purple flowers. This hybrid and its cultivars are sterile and cannot be grown from seed. 'Dawn to Dusk' has pink flowers. 'Dropmore' has gray-green foliage and light purple flowers. 'Snowflake' is low growing, compact and spreading with white flowers. It grows 12–24" tall and spreads about 18". 'Walker's Low' has gray-green foliage and bears lavender blue flowers. It grows about 10" tall.

N. 'Six Hills Giant' is a large, vigorous plant about 36" tall and about 24" in spread. It bears large, showy spikes of deep lavender blue flowers.

Problems & Pests

These plants are pest free, except for an occasional cat or bout of leaf spot.

It is no mystery where the name 'catmint' comes from—cats love it! Dried leaves stuffed into cloth toys will amuse your kitty for hours.

'Walker's Low.'

Chrysanthemum
Fall Garden Mum, Hybrid Garden Mum
Chrysanthemum

Height: 12–36" **Spread:** 1–4' **Flower color:** orange, yellow, pink, red, purple, white **Blooms:** late summer and fall **Zones:** 5–9

NOTHING PERKS UP THE FALL GARDEN LIKE FLOWERING MUMS, and because they come in a wide variety of colors and shapes, they work well in any scheme. Unless you choose to treat these pretties as annuals, pinching, dividing and careful timing are part of successful overwintering. Planting small transplants in spring allows them to become established over the growing season. Remove any buds or flowers before planting, but give the young plants a couple of weeks before pinching back. When established mums reach 6" in height, I cut them back to 4". To expand my collection, I root these cuttings in soil-less potting mix. It takes but a few weeks.

Planting

Seeding: Not recommended

Planting out: Spring, summer, fall

Spacing: 18–24"

Growing

Chrysanthemums grow best in **full sun**. The soil should be **fertile, moist** and **well drained**. Divide in spring or fall every two years to keep plants vigorous and to prevent them from thinning out in the center.

Pinch plants back in early summer to encourage bushy growth. In late fall or early winter, you can deadhead the spent blooms, but leave the stems intact to protect the crowns.

The earlier in the season you can plant chrysanthemums, the better. Early planting improves their chances of surviving the winter.

'Raquel' (below)

'Christine' (above)

Tips

These plants provide a blaze of color in the late-season garden, often flowering until the first hard frost. Dot or group them in borders or use them as specimen plants near the house or in large planters. Some gardeners purchase chrysanthemums as flowering plants in late summer and put them in the spots where summer annuals have faded.

Recommended

C. 'Morden' series was developed in Canada and is hardy to Zone 4. Plants come in a wide variety of colors and grow about 24" tall.

C. 'My Favorite' series is a new introduction and is heralded as a truly perennial mum and a prolific flower producer. The plants grow to about 24" tall and spread about 4'.

'**Autumn Red**' is one cultivar in the series; it has red flowers.

C. '**Prophet**' series is popular and commonly available. Plants grow about 24" tall and spread about 24–36". Flowers come in all colors. '**Christine**' has deep salmon pink double flowers with yellow centers. '**Raquel**' has bright red double flowers with yellow centers. '**Stacy**' has yellow-centered flowers with pink petals that have white bases.

Problems & Pests

Aphids can be a true menace to these plants. Insecticidal soap can be used to treat the problem, but it should be washed off within an hour because it discolors the foliage when the sun hits it. Also watch for spider mites, whiteflies, leaf miners, leaf spot, powdery mildew, rust, aster yellows, blight, borers and rot, though these problems are not as common.

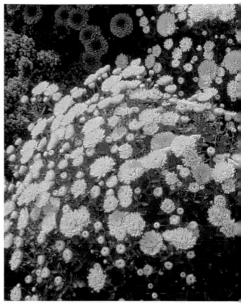

'Stacy' (below)

Clematis
Clematis

Height: 18"–16' **Spread:** 2–4' **Flower color:** blue, purple, pink, yellow, red, white **Blooms:** summer **Zones:** 3–8

NOTHING IS MORE BREATHTAKING THAN A CLEMATIS vine in full bloom. By choosing the right varieties, you can enjoy an incredible show of color in your garden from spring through fall—and there is no rule that says these colorful vines must be grown on trellises and lampposts. Lovers of old-fashioned roses that bloom once a season can thread these lovely flowering vines through the rose bushes to extend the season of color. Less well known and not quite as showy, but certainly worth investigating, are the non-climbing species that reach heights of only 3–4'. Solitary Clematis forms an urn shape that is covered with small purple-blue bells for several weeks in late summer, followed by a shower of fuzzy seedheads.

Planting
Seeding: Indoors or in a cold frame, in late summer or fall

Planting out: Spring or fall

Spacing: 2–4'

Growing

Clematis prefer **full sun** but tolerate partial shade. The soil should be **fertile, humus rich, moist** and **well drained**. These plants are quite cold hardy but will fare best when protected from the winter wind. The rootball of vining clematis should be planted 2" beneath the surface of the soil. Dividing is difficult and not recommended, but herbaceous clematis may be divided in early spring. Vining clematis can be propagated by taking stem cuttings in summer.

The semi-woody, vine-type clematis need to be pruned. Those that bloom in early summer on last year's growth should be thinned after the bloom by pruning lateral branches back to three or four nodes. Mid- to late-season varieties that bloom on the current year's growth, such as Jackman Clematis, 'Comtesse de Bouchard' and 'Ramona,' should be pruned back to 1' early in spring before new growth appears. Large mid-season varieties that bloom on year-old wood and then again on new growth, such as 'Nellie Moser,' 'The President' and 'Duchess of Edinburgh,' should be thinned

Combine two clematis varieties that bloom at the same time to provide a mix of tone and texture.

C. recta

C. *integrifolia* (above),
C. x *jackmanii* (below)

occasionally after the vine ceases its
first round of blooms.

Tips

Clematis are attractive for most of the
growing season. They are useful in
borders and as specimen plants.
Vine-type clematis need a structure
like a trellis, railing, fence or arbor to
support them as they climb. They can
also be allowed to grow over shrubs,
up trees and as groundcovers.

Shade the roots with a mulch or
groundcover. Do not shade with a
flat rock, which was a common prac-
tice in the past, because the rock will
absorb heat and defeat the purpose
of shading the roots.

Recommended

C. '**Comtesse de Bouchard**' is a mid-
to late-summer bloomer that bears
mauve pink flowers. It grows about
10' tall.

C. '**Duchess of Edinburgh**' is an
early-summer bloomer that bears
white double flowers. It grows about
10' tall.

C. '**Gravetye Beauty**' is a late-season
bloomer about 8' tall. Its small,
bright red flowers bloom on new
growth.

C. heracleifolia (Tube Clematis)
grows up to 3' tall and 4' wide. The
tube-shaped flowers are purple-blue.
Var. *davidiana* has fragrant, larger
flowers. Cut these plants back to the
ground in early spring. Pinch plants
when they are 15" tall to promote
upright growth.

C. integrifolia (Solitary Clematis)
grows 18–36" tall and bears flared,
bell-like, purple flowers. It tends

to grow upwards to a point, then falls to the ground and sprawls for up to 4'. Stake in spring to help keep this colorful character upright.

C. x *jackmanii* (Jackman Clematis) is a common mid- to late summer bloomer. The twining vines of this hybrid grow about 10' tall. Large, purple flowers appear on side shoots from the previous season and on new growth for most of the summer.

C. 'Nelly Moser' is a popular early-summer bloomer that grows about 10' tall. It bears pale mauve pink flowers with a darker pink stripe down the center of each petal.

C. 'The President' blooms in early summer and bears dark purple flowers. It grows about 15' tall.

C. 'Ramona' is a mid-summer bloomer that bears pale purple-blue flowers and grows about 10' tall.

C. recta (Ground Clematis) is a bit more upright than the other two species. It reaches 4' in height and only 24" in width. The fragrant white flowers are borne in dense clusters. The cultivar 'Purpurea' has red-tinged leaves and white flowers. Cut these plants back after flowering for a flush of new growth.

C. tangutica (Virgin's Bower) is a late-season bloomer that reaches 16' or more in height. Its great capacity for spreading makes it a good choice on a chain-link fence, where it will fill in thickly and create a privacy screen. The nodding yellow flowers of this species are followed by particularly distinctive fuzzy seedheads that persist into winter.

Problems & Pests

Problems with scale insects, whiteflies, aphids, wilt, powdery mildew, rust, leaf spot and stem canker can occur. To avoid wilt, keep mulch from touching the stem. Protect the fragile stems of newly planted clematis from injury; a bruised or damaged stem is an entry point for disease.

The fuzzy seedheads of some species gave rise to the alternative common name 'old man's beard.'

C. integrifolia

Columbine
Aquilegia

Height: 9–36" **Spread:** 12–18" **Flower color:** red, yellow, pink, purple, blue, white; color of spurs often differs from that of petals **Blooms:** spring, summer **Zones:** 2–9

IT MAY BE HARD TO BELIEVE that one of these colorful, exotic-looking, spring-blooming species is a native of Michigan and that it's a snap to grow. Mother Nature plants our Wild Columbine at the edges of woodlands, so although it will grow in sunny gardens, it is happier if provided afternoon shade. Cultivated varieties come in a wide range of colors, so columbines work well in any color scheme. In a mixed border, pair them with False Indigo, any of the catmints, Creeping Phlox or Cranesbill Geranium. As warm weather arrives, squiggly white lines caused by leaf miners may appear on the leaves but are not a problem for the plant. These deer-resistant love-lies attract hummingbirds, so if you plant them, hang that hummingbird feeder out early in spring.

Planting

Seeding: Direct sow in spring

Planting out: Spring

Spacing: 18"

Growing

Columbines grow well in **full sun** or **partial shade**. They prefer soil that is **fertile, moist** and **well drained** but adapt well to most soil conditions. These plants self-seed, and young seedlings can be transplanted. Division is not required but can be done to propagate desirable plants. The divided plants may take a while to recover because they dislike having their roots disturbed.

Tips

Use columbines in a rock garden, a formal or casual border, or in a naturalized or woodland garden.

Columbines self-seed but are in no way invasive. Each year a few new plants may turn up near the parent plant. If you have a variety of columbines planted near each other,

A. vulgaris 'Nora Barlow' (above)

you may even wind up with a new hybrid, because these plants cross-breed easily. The wide variety of flower colors is the most interesting result. The new seedlings may not be identical to the parents and there is some chance they will revert to the original species.

Recommended

A. canadensis (Wild Columbine, Canada Columbine) is native to most of eastern North America and is common in woodlands and fields. It grows up to 24" tall, spreads about 12" and bears yellow flowers with red spurs.

A. x *hybrida* (*A.* x *cultorum*) (Hybrid Columbine) forms mounds of delicate foliage and has exceptional flowers. Many groups of hybrids have been developed for their showy flowers in a wide range of colors. When the parentage of a columbine

'McKana Giants' (above), *A.* x *hybrida* (below)

is uncertain, it is grouped under this name. **'Biedermeier'** is a compact variety, growing 9–12" tall with white, purple or pink flowers. **'Double Pleat'** (Double Pleat Hybrids) includes plants that grow 30–32" tall and bear double flowers in combinations of blue and white or pink and white. **'Dragonfly'** (Dragonfly Hybrids) includes compact plants up to 24" tall and 12" in spread, with a wide range of flower colors. **'McKana Giants'** (McKana Hybrids) are popular and bear flowers in yellow, pink, red, purple, mauve and white. They grow up to 36" tall.

A. vulgaris (European Columbine, Common Columbine) grows about 36" tall and spreads 18". Flowers come in a wide variety of colors, and this species has been used to develop many hybrids and cultivars. **'Nora Barlow'** is a popular cultivar with double flowers in white, pink and green-tinged red.

Problems & Pests

Mildew and rust can be troublesome during dry weather. Other problems include fungal leaf spot, aphids, caterpillars and leaf miners.

'McKana Giants' (this page)

Columbines are short-lived perennials that seed freely, establishing themselves in unexpected, and often charming, locations. If you wish to keep a particular form, you must preserve it carefully through frequent division or root cuttings.

Coral Bells
Alum Root
Heuchera

Height: 1–4' **Spread:** 12–18" **Flower color:** red, pink, white, purple
Blooms: spring, summer **Zones:** 3–9

CORAL BELLS ARE OLD-FASHIONED PERENNIALS that were paid little attention until the colorful and now famous bronze-leaved 'Palace Purple' made its debut several years ago. It became the darling of the shade-garden crowd, and now there are dozens of varieties to choose from, with leaves that may be burgundy, burgundy-veined, metallic pewter or variegated. Though foliage is the focus of these new kids on the block, some recent introductions, such as 'White Cloud,' 'June Bride' and 'Firefly,' also feature improved flowers. I still have one of the varieties from Grandma's era in my garden, a gift that I treasure from a dear departed neighbor. The humming-birds love it and the deer don't, making it an undisputed winner in my book.

Planting

Seeding: Species, but not cultivars, may be started from seed in spring in a cold frame

Planting out: Spring

Spacing: 12–18"

Growing

Coral bells grow best in **light or partial shade.** Foliage colors can bleach out in full sun and plants become leggy in full shade. The soil should be of **average to rich fertility, humus rich, neutral to alkaline, moist** and **well drained**. Good air circulation is essential.

The spent flowers should be removed to prolong the blooming period. Every two or three years coral bells should be dug up to remove the oldest, woodiest roots and stems. Plants may be divided at this time, if desired, then replanted with the crown at or just above soil level. Cultivars may be propagated by division in spring or fall.

H. micrantha var. diversifolia
'Palace Purple'

Tips

Use coral bells as edging plants, in clusters in woodland gardens or as groundcovers in low traffic areas. Combine different foliage types for an interesting display.

Cut flowers of Heuchera (hew-ker-uh) species can be used in fresh arrangements.

H. sanguinea

Coral bells have a strange habit of pushing themselves up out of the soil. Mulch in fall if the plants begin heaving from the ground.

Recommended

Most of the cultivars listed are hybrids developed from crosses between the various species. They are grouped with one of their acknowledged parents in the following list.

H. americana is a mound-forming plant about 18" tall and 12" in spread. Its heart-shaped foliage is marbled and bronze-veined when it is young and matures to deep green. Cultivars have been developed for their attractive and variable foliage. **'Chocolate Veil'** has dark chocolaty purple leaves with silvery patches between the veins. Its flowers are greenish purple. **'Pewter Veil'** has silvery purple leaves with dark gray veins. Its flowers are white flushed with pink.

H. x brizoides is a group of mound-forming hybrids developed for their attractive flowers. They grow 12–30" tall and spread 12–18". **'Firefly'** has fragrant, bright pinkish red flowers. **'June Bride'** has large, white flowers. **'Raspberry Regal'** is a larger plant, growing up to 4' tall. The foliage is strongly marbled and the flowers are bright red.

H. micrantha is a mounding, clump-forming plant up to 36" tall. The foliage is gray-green and the flowers are white. The species is not common in gardens, but many cultivars are very common. **'Bressingham Hybrids'** are compact hybrids that can be started from seed. The flowers are pink or red. **'Chocolate Ruffles'** has ruffled, glossy, brown foliage with purple undersides that give the leaves a bronzed appearance. **Var.** *diversifolia* **'Palace Purple'** is one of the best known cultivars of all the coral bells. This compact cultivar has deep purple foliage and

H. americana cultivar

white blooms. It grows 18–20" tall. It can be started from seed, but only some of the seedlings will be true to type. **'Pewter Moon'** has light pink flowers and silvery leaves with bronzy purple veins.

H. sanguinea is the hardiest species. It forms a low-growing mat of foliage. It grows 12–18" tall, with an equal spread. The dark green foliage is marbled with silver. The red, pink or white flowers are borne in summer. **'Coral Cloud'** has pinkish red flowers and glossy, crinkled leaves. **'Frosty'** has red flowers and silver-variegated foliage. **'Northern Fire'** has red flowers and leaves mottled with silver. **'White Cloud'** has silver-mottled leaves and bears white flowers in late spring.

Problems & Pests

Healthy coral bells have very few problems. In stressed situations, they can be afflicted with foliar nematodes, powdery mildew, rust or leaf spot.

H. x brizoides 'Firefly' (above), *H. m.* var. *diversifolia* 'Palace Purple' (below)

These delicate woodland plants will enhance your garden with their bright colors, attractive foliage and airy sprays of flowers.

Coreopsis
Tickseed
Coreopsis

Height: 6–36" **Spread:** 12–24" **Flower color:** yellow, pink, orange
Blooms: summer **Zones:** 3–9

OF ALL THE FLOWERS IN THE PERENNIAL GARDEN, none works harder than the coreopsis. They're long blooming, brightly colored and easy to grow. Plants range in size from the dainty-flowered, 9" 'Nana' to the showy, double-flowered, 3' 'Mayfield Giant.' Constant deadheading is the secret to extended bloom, and fast-draining soils are needed for the plants to over-winter. Even with all the right conditions, many rarely live beyond three years—some say they just bloom themselves to death. Still, you get a big bang for your buck during their short stay in the garden.

Planting

Seeding: Direct sow in spring. Seeds may be sown indoors in winter, but soil must be kept fairly cool, at 55–61° F, in order for seeds to germinate.

Planting out: Spring

Spacing: 12–18"

Growing

Grow coreopsis in **full sun**. The soil should be **average, sandy, light** and **well drained**. Plants can develop crown rot in moist, cool locations with heavy soil. Overly fertile soil causes long, floppy growth. Frequent division may be required to keep plants vigorous.

Deadhead daily to keep plants in constant summer bloom. Use scissors to snip out tall stems. Shear plants by one-half in late spring for more compact growth.

C. grandiflora cultivar (above), *C. verticillata* 'Moonbeam' (below)

Mass plant coreopsis to fill in a dry, exposed bank where nothing else will grow, and you will enjoy the bright, sunny flowers all summer long.

C. verticillata (above), C. rosea (below)

Tips

Coreopsis are versatile plants, useful in formal and informal borders and in meadow plantings or cottage gardens. They look best in groups.

Recommended

C. auriculata (Mouse-eared Tickseed) is low growing and well suited to rock gardens or fronts of borders. It grows 12–24" tall and will continue to creep outwards without becoming invasive. **'Nana'** grows 6–9" tall and bears orange-yellow flowers in late spring.

C. grandiflora (Large-flowered Coreopsis, Tickseed) forms a clump

of foliage and bears bright golden yellow flowers over a long period in mid- and late summer. It grows 18–36" tall and spreads 12–18". This species and its cultivars are often grown as annuals because bearing so many flowers leaves them with little energy for surviving the winter. '**Early Sunrise**' is a compact plant that grows 18–24" tall. It bears double yellow flowers and can be started from seed. '**Mayfield Giant**' bears large, bright yellow flowers on plants up to 36" tall.

C. rosea (Pink Tickseed) is an unusual species with pink flowers. It grows 24" tall and 12" wide. This species is more shade and water tolerant than the other species, but it is not as vigorous.

C. verticillata (Thread-leaf Coreopsis) is a mound-forming plant with attractive, finely divided foliage. It grows 24–32" tall and spreads 18". This long-lived species needs to be divided less frequently than most others. Divide if some of the plant seems to be dying out. '**Golden Showers**' has large, golden yellow flowers and fern-like foliage. '**Moonbeam**' forms a compact mound of delicate foliage. The flowers are a light, creamy yellow.

Problems & Pests

Occasional problems with slugs, bacterial spot, gray mold, aster yellows, powdery mildew, downy mildew, crown rot and fungal spot are possible.

C. grandiflora 'Early Sunrise'

Cornflower
Mountain Bluet
Centaurea

Height: 12–24" **Spread:** 12–24" or more **Flower color:** blue, purple, pink, white **Blooms:** late spring to mid-summer **Zones:** 3–8

THERE'S SOMETHING MAGICAL ABOUT BLUE FLOWERS, and in my garden the gorgeous perennial Cornflower puts on a great show in spring and early summer. After about two years this blue rogue became aggressive, so now I dig it out in fall. I never get all the creeping roots, so it comes roaring back in spring, but it remains a reasonable size. A number of cultivars and related species bear showy white, pink or amethyst flowers and are better behaved. As the demand for these plants increases, we should see some interesting imports appear on the scene.

Planting

Seeding: Direct sow in late summer; protect seedlings first winter

Planting out: Spring

Spacing: 24"

Growing

Cornflower grows well in **full sun** or **light shade**. The soil should be of **poor or average fertility, moist** and **well drained**. In a rich soil, plants may develop straggly, floppy growth and may become invasive. Divide in spring or late summer every two or three years.

Deadhead to prolong blooming and to prevent self-sowing. Use a bed-edging material or a bottomless flowerpot to surround the plant and limit its spread.

Tips

Cornflower makes an attractive addition to borders, informal or natural gardens and large rock gardens.

Thin the new shoots by about one-third in spring to increase air circulation through the plant.

Recommended

C. montana is a mounding or sprawling plant that bears bright cobalt blue flowers from late spring until mid-summer. Plants may self-seed. 'Alba' bears white flowers. 'Carnea' ('Rosea') bears pink flowers.

Problems & Pests

Rare problems with downy or powdery mildew, rust or mold can occur.

Prompt deadheading, by cutting spent blooms back to lateral buds, extends the bloom. For more flowers in late summer, cut plants back to the basal growth as soon as blooming ceases.

Crocosmia
Crocosmia

Height: 18"–4' **Spread:** 12–18" **Flower color:** red, orange, yellow
Blooms: mid- to late summer **Zones:** 5–9

A UNIQUE AND ARCHITECTURALLY INTERESTING FORM combined with intense red-hot color makes a flowering 'Lucifer' a showstopper in any garden from mid-July through August. When the big show is over, these self-cleaning blooms slowly fade and drop away, leaving seed capsules that add an interesting twist as they develop. In hot color schemes, match 'Lucifer' with sneezeweeds and goldenrods and one of the taller coreopsis.

Planting

Seeding: Start indoors or out in early spring

Planting out: Spring

Spacing: 8"

Some people still know crocosmias by the older name, montbretia. The new name comes from the Greek words krokos, *'saffron,' and* osme, *'smell,' referring to the saffron-like scent of the dried flowers when placed in water.*

Growing

Crocosmias prefer **full sun**. The soil should be of **average fertility, humus rich, moist** and **well drained**. Plant in a protected area and provide a good mulch of shredded leaves or other organic matter in fall to protect the roots from fluctuating winter temperatures. Every two or three years, whenever the clump is dense, divide in spring before growth starts. Overgrown clumps produce fewer flowers.

Tips

These attractive and unusual plants create a striking display when planted in clumps in a herbaceous or mixed border. They look good when planted next to a pond where the brightly colored flowers can reflect off the surface of the water.

Recommended

C. x *crocosmiflora* is a spreading plant with long, strap-like foliage. It grows 18–36" tall and the clump spreads about 12". One-sided spikes of red, orange or yellow flowers are borne in mid- and late summer. **'Citronella'** ('Golden Fleece') bears bright yellow flowers.

C. **'Lucifer'** is the hardiest of the bunch and bears bright red flowers. It grows 3–4' tall, with a spread of about 18".

Problems & Pests

Occasional trouble with spider mites can occur. Hose the mites off as soon as they appear.

If your garden is too cold in winter for crocosmias, don't despair. Dig up the corms in fall and store them in slightly damp sawdust or peat moss in a cool, dark place. Check on them regularly and when they start to sprout, pot them and move them to a well-lit room until they can be planted out.

Daylily
Hemerocallis

Height: 1– 4' **Spread:** 2– 4' or more **Flower color:** every color except blue and pure white **Blooms:** summer **Zones:** 2–9

IF YOU'RE YEARNING FOR A PLANT THAT IS PRETTY as a picture, yet sturdy as a tank, the daylilies are your dream come true. And choosing a range of cultivars will keep the color coming most of the summer. 'Stella d'Oro,' a short variety with egg-yolk-colored blossoms, is the champion of the re-bloomers, flowering sporadically all summer. 'Happy Returns,' which sports slightly larger, softer yellow blooms, is another marathon re-bloomer. For a contrast in textures, group your daylilies with 'Six Hills Giant' catmint, Russian Sage and 'Johnson's Blue' geranium. In a partly shaded garden, try partnering daylilies with ferns, hostas and colorful coral bells.

Planting

Seeding: Not recommended; hybrids and cultivars don't come true to type

Planting out: Spring

Spacing: 1–4'

Growing

Daylilies grow in any light from **full sun** to **full shade**. The deeper the shade, the fewer flowers will be produced. The soil should be **fertile, moist** and **well drained,** but these plants adapt to most conditions and are hard to kill once established. Feed your daylilies in spring and mid-summer to produce the best display of blooms. Divide every two to three years to keep plants vigorous and to propagate them. They can be left indefinitely without dividing.

Tips

Plant daylilies alone, or group them in borders, on banks and in ditches

Derived from the Greek words for day, hemera, *and beauty,* kallos, *the genus name, like the common name, indicates that each lovely bloom lasts for only one day.*

to control erosion. They can be naturalized in woodland or meadow gardens. Small varieties are nice in planters.

Deadhead small varieties to keep them blooming as long as possible. Be careful when deadheading purple-flowered daylilies, because the sap can stain fingers and clothes.

Recommended

You can find an almost infinite number of forms, sizes and colors in a range of species, cultivars and hybrids. See your local garden center or daylily grower to find out what's available and most suitable for your garden. Several commonly available and attractive daylilies are listed here.

H. citrina (Citron Daylily, Lemon Daylily) bears very fragrant, yellow flowers that open in the evening. It grows up to 4' tall and spreads about 2'.

H. fulva (Tawny Daylily, Orange Daylily) is a large, often invasive plant that has naturalized in

most of eastern North America. It bears orange flowers for a long period in mid- and late summer. It grows 3–4' tall and can spread 2–4' or more. This plant is often seen growing in ditches alongside roads.

H. '**Happy Returns**' bears yellow flowers for most of the summer. It grows about 16" tall.

H. '**Stella d'Oro**' is another repeat bloomer. The bright, golden yellow flowers appear on modest-sized 12" plants.

Problems & Pests

Generally these plants are pest free. Rare problems with rust, *Hemerocallis* gall midge, aphids, spider mites, thrips and slugs are possible.

H. fulva cultivar (above)

Dead Nettle
Spotted Dead Nettle, Lamium
Lamium

Height: 4–24" **Spread:** indefinite **Flower color:** white, pink, yellow, mauve; plant also grown for foliage **Blooms:** spring, summer **Zones:** 3–8

WHEN IT COMES TO GROUNDCOVERS, if you're tired of the same old choices and are looking for a colorful change, start a collection of dead nettles. They may not have a pretty name, but they're gorgeous plants. Dead nettles will shine in the shade garden, with their stunning variegated leaves in combinations of frosted silver, bright green and lime. To top it off, they bear delicate bunches of tiny, snapdragon-like, pink, purple or white flowers. The long-blooming and showy 'Orchid Frost,' discovered right here in Michigan by Mike Bovio of English Gardens, is a favorite for gardens and containers alike.

Planting

Seeding: Not recommended; cultivars don't come true to type

Planting out: Spring

Spacing: 12–24"

Growing

Dead nettles prefer **partial to light shade.** They tolerate full sun but may become leggy. The soil should be of **average fertility, humus rich, moist** and **well drained.** The more fertile the soil, the more vigorously the plants will grow. These plants are drought tolerant when grown in the shade but can develop bare patches if the soil is allowed to dry out for extended periods. Divide and re-plant in fall if bare spots become unsightly.

Dead nettles remain more compact if sheared back after flowering.

Dead nettles are so named because their leaves resemble those of stinging nettle but have no sting.

L. galeobdolon 'Florentinum'

Tips

These plants can be useful groundcovers for woodland or shade gardens or under shrubs in a border, where the dead nettles can keep weeds down.

Keep in mind that dead nettles can be quite invasive and are likely to overwhelm less vigorous plants. If your dead nettles become invasive, pull some of them up, making sure to remove the fleshy roots.

Recommended

L. maculatum is a low-growing, spreading species that grows 8" tall and spreads at least 36". The green leaves often have white or silvery markings. White, pink or mauve flowers are borne in summer. **'Anne Greenaway'** has green leaves with gold margins and silver centers. It bears light purple flowers in spring. **'Aureum'** has gold or yellow foliage with white-striped centers. Its flowers are pink. **'Beacon Silver'** has green-edged, silver foliage and pink flowers. **'Chequers'** has green leaves with silver stripes down the centers. The flowers are mauve. **'Orchid Frost'** has silvery

L. galeobdolon 'Florentinum' (this page)

foliage with green margins. It bears deep pink flowers on 4–6" stems. **'White Nancy'** has white flowers and silver leaves with green margins.

Alternate Species

L. galeobdolon (White Archangel) can be quite invasive, though the cultivars are less so. It grows 12–24" tall and spreads indefinitely. The flowers are yellow. **'Florentinum'** ('Variegatum') has silver foliage with green margins. **'Silver Angel'** is a prostrate cultivar with silvery foliage.

Problems & Pests

Rare problems with slugs, powdery mildew, downy mildew and leaf spot are possible.

L. maculatum
'Beacon Silver' (above)

Delphinium
Candle Delphinium, Candle Larkspur
Delphinium

Height: 8"–6' or more **Spread:** 12–36" **Flower color:** blue, purple, pink, white, yellow or bicolors **Blooms:** late spring, early summer **Zones:** 3–7

WHEN IT COMES TO SPECTACULAR COLOR IN THE GARDEN, delphiniums are truly over the top, and if you have the right soil conditions, they will treat you to a sumptuous summer-long display. The giants that tower to 6' or more are spectacular, but some of the shorter varieties, such as the 'Magic Fountain' series, are probably better suited to the smaller home garden. These plants are heavy feeders that require rich soil with impeccable drainage in order to make an encore appearance the following year. To avoid frustration, many gardeners treat them as fabulous flowering annuals.

Planting

Seeding: Seeds direct sown in spring will produce flowers the following year. Seedlings may not be true to type.

Planting out: Spring or fall. Plant with crown at soil level to avoid crown rot.

Spacing: 24"

Growing

Grow in a **full sun** location that is well protected from strong winds. The soil should be **fertile, moist** and **humus rich** with **excellent drainage**. Delphiniums love well-composted manure mixed into the soil. These heavy feeders require fertilizer twice a year, in spring and summer. Delphiniums require division each year, in spring, to keep them vigorous.

To encourage a second flush of smaller blooms, remove the first flower spikes once they begin to fade and before they begin to set seed. Cut them off just above the foliage. New shoots will begin to grow and the old foliage will fade back. The old growth may then be cut right back, allowing new growth to fill in.

Tips

Delphiniums are classic cottage-garden plants. Their height and

D. x *elatum* (this page)

Delphis *is the Greek word for dolphin, which lends itself well to this flower: the petals of the flowers resemble the nose and fins of a dolphin.*

need for staking relegate them to the back of the border, where they make a magnificent blue-toned backdrop for warmer foreground flowers such as peonies, poppies and black-eyed Susans.

The tall flower spikes of many delphiniums have hollow centers and break easily if exposed to the wind. Each flower spike needs to be individually staked. Stakes should be installed as soon as the flower spike reaches 12" in height. You can use a wire tomato cage for a clump.

D. x *belladonna* (above), *D.* x *elatum* (below)

Recommended

D. x *belladonna* (Belladonna Hybrids) bears flowers of blue, white or mauve in loose, branched spikes. It grows 3–4' tall and spreads 12–18". '**Blue Bees**' has pale blue flowers with white centers. '**Wendy**' has dark purple-blue flowers.

D. x *elatum* (Elatum Hybrids) bears densely clustered flowers of blue, purple, white, pink or yellow on tall spikes. This group of hybrids is divided into three height categories: dwarf plants grow up to 5', medium plants grow 5–6' and tall plants grow over 6'. All spread about 36". '**Blue Dawn**' has blue flowers with dark blue centers. '**Magic Fountain**' series bears flowers in a variety of colors on plants that grow 24–36" tall. '**Turkish Delight**' has pink flowers with white centers.

D. grandiflorum (*D. chinense*) bears flowers of blue, purple or white in loose, branched clusters. It grows 8–20" tall and spreads up to 12". '**Album**' has white flowers. '**Blue Butterfly**' bears bright blue flowers on compact plants.

Problems & Pests

Problems can be caused by slugs, powdery mildew, bacterial and fungal leaf spot, gray mold, crown and root rot, white rot, rust, white smut, leaf smut and damping off. Although this is a daunting list, remember that healthy plants are less susceptible to problems.

These plants are so gorgeous in bloom that you can build a garden or plan a party around their flowering.

D. x *elatum* 'Magic Fountain'

Euphorbia
Cushion Spurge
Euphorbia

Height: 12–24" **Spread:** 12–24" **Flower color:** yellow, green, orange
Blooms: spring to mid-summer **Zones:** 4–9

EUPHORBIAS, WITH THEIR GLOWING GREEN-GOLD BRACTS, were considered ho hum for decades until trendy garden designers swept them up to use as accents with other colorful foliage plants. These deer-resistant, season-long workhorses color up in spring and keep on going. 'Chameleon' produces mounds of rich purple foliage that, in spring, is covered with loose clusters of yellow-green or orange flowers and bracts. It looks especially lovely alongside perennials with blue flowers and silver foliage.

Planting

Seeding: Use fresh seed for best germination rates. Start seed in cold frame in spring.

Planting out: Spring or fall

Spacing: 18"

Growing

Euphorbias grow well in **full sun** or **light shade**. The soil should be of **average fertility, moist, humus rich** and **well drained**. These plants are drought tolerant and can be invasive in a too-fertile soil. Euphorbias can be propagated by stem cuttings and they may self-seed in the garden. Division is rarely required. These plants dislike being disturbed once established.

Tips

Use euphorbias in a mixed or herbaceous border, rock garden or lightly shaded woodland garden.

If you are cutting the stems for propagation, dip the cut ends in hot water before planting to stop the sticky white sap from running.

E. polychroma (above),
E. dulcis 'Chameleon' (below)

E. *polychroma* (this page)

Don't confuse these euphorbias with the invasive, weedy Leafy Spurge *(E. esula)*. Leafy Spurge is rarely sold in garden centers, but it is common at perennial exchanges and should be strenuously avoided.

Recommended

E. dulcis is a compact, upright plant that grows about 12" tall, with an equal spread. The spring flowers and bracts are yellow-green. The dark bronze-green leaves turn red and orange in fall. **'Chameleon'** has purple-red foliage that turns darker purple in fall. There appear to be two plants in garden centers sharing the same cultivar name. Both have the purple foliage, but depending on where you shop, you may find yourself with an orange-flowered or a purple-tinged, yellowish-green-flowered 'Chameleon.' Ask before you buy.

E. polychroma (E. epithimoides) (Cushion Spurge) is a mounding, clump-forming plant 12–24" tall and 18–24" in spread. The inconspicuous flowers are surrounded by long-lasting yellow bracts. The foliage turns shades of purple, red or orange in fall. There are several cultivars, though the species is more commonly available. **'Candy'** has yellow bracts and flowers, and the leaves and stems are tinged with purple. **'Emerald Jade'** is a compact plant that grows to 14" in height. The bracts are yellow and the flowers are bright green.

You may wish to wear gloves when handling these plants; some people find the milky sap irritates their skin. Many euphorbias are also toxic if ingested.

Problems & Pests

Aphids, spider mites and nematodes are possible problems, along with fungal root rot in poorly drained, wet soil.

False Indigo
Baptisia

Height: 3–5' **Spread:** 2–4' **Flower color:** purple-blue
Blooms: late spring, early summer **Zones:** 3–9

BECAUSE FALSE INDIGO TAKES THREE TO FOUR YEARS to mature, a lot of gardeners have overlooked this striking contender for the late-spring garden. A native of Michigan, it's a wonderful addition to a wildflower bed or to a perennial border with peonies, poppies and irises. Once established, this tough cookie is unfazed by drought and heat and resents disturbance, so it doesn't need dividing. Pair it with yarrows, columbines, roses or other June bloomers, and enjoy.

Planting

Seeding: Sow indoors in early spring or direct sow in late summer. Protect plants for the first winter.

Planting out: Spring

Spacing: 24–36"

Growing

False Indigo prefers **full sun** but tolerates partial shade. Too much shade results in lank growth that causes the plant to split and fall. The soil should be of **average or poor fertility, sandy** and **well drained**. Divide carefully in spring, only when you desire more plants.

Staking may be required if the plant is not getting enough sun. Rather than worry about staking or having to move the plant, place it in the sun and give it lots of space to spread.

The hard seed coats may need to be penetrated before the seeds can germinate. Scratch the seeds between two pieces of sandpaper before planting them.

Tips

False Indigo can be used in an informal border or cottage-type garden. It is attractive when used in a natural planting, on a slope, or in any well-drained, sunny spot in the garden.

Recommended

B. australis is an upright or rather spreading, clump-forming plant that bears spikes of purple-blue flowers in early summer.

Problems & Pests

Minor problems with mildew, leaf spot and rust can occur.

If you've had difficulties with lupines, try growing the far less demanding False Indigo instead.

False Sunflower
Ox Eye, Orange Sunflower
Heliopsis

Height: 3–5' **Spread:** 18–36" **Flower color:** yellow, orange
Blooms: mid-summer to mid-fall **Zones:** 2–9

IF FLOWERS SEND MESSAGES, False Sunflower sings out, 'It's fun in the sun!' This hardy Michigan native blooms from mid-summer into fall and can be found gracing roadsides and meadows. Planting named varieties will allow you to enjoy more compact growth and to select your choice of single, semi-double or double flower forms. Combine these bright characters with Shasta Daisy, Blazing Star, butterfly weeds, asters and ornamental grasses.

The stems of False Sunflower are stiff, making the blooms useful in fresh arrangements.

Planting

Seeding: Start seed in spring, with soil temperature at about 68° F

Planting out: Spring

Spacing: 24"

Growing

False Sunflower prefers **full sun** but tolerates partial shade. The soil should be **average to fertile, humus rich, moist** and **well drained**. Most soil conditions are tolerated, including poor, dry soils. Divide every two or so years.

Deadhead to prolong the blooming period. Cut plants back once flowering is complete.

Tips

Use False Sunflower at the back or in the middle of mixed or herbaceous borders. This plant is easy to grow and popular with novice gardeners.

Recommended

H. helianthoides forms an upright clump of stems and foliage and bears yellow or orange, daisy-like flowers. **'Summer Sun'** ('Sommersonne') bears single or semi-double flowers in bright golden yellow. It grows about 36" tall.

Problems & Pests

Occasional trouble with aphids and powdery mildew can occur.

This plant is native to most of eastern North America.

Foamflower
Tiarella

Height: 4–12" **Spread:** 12–24" **Flower color:** white, pink
Blooms: spring, sometimes to early summer **Zones:** 3–8

THESE DEER-RESISTANT PLANTS make a charming addition to any
woodland garden. In spring, foamflowers form small clumps of attractive
maple-like foliage and produce clusters of tiny, white or pink flowers that
from a distance look like spikes of airy foam. The lovely evergreen foliage
fills in rapidly with a strawberry-like growth habit, making an interesting
textured carpet for ferns, hostas and astilbes. Many of the newer varieties
are variegated, textured or veined with cream, black and shades of green
and burgundy.

Planting

Seeding: Start seed in
cold frame in spring

Planting out: Spring

Spacing: 6–24"

Growing

Foamflowers prefer **partial, light or full shade** without afternoon sun. The soil should be **humus rich, moist** and **slightly acidic**. These plants adapt to most soils. Divide in spring. Deadhead to encourage re-blooming.

If the foliage fades or rusts in summer, cut it partway to the ground and new growth will emerge.

Tips

Foamflowers are excellent groundcovers for shaded and woodland gardens. They can be included in shaded borders and left to naturalize in wild gardens.

These plants spread by underground stems, which are easily pulled up to stop excessive spread.

Recommended

T. cordifolia is a low-growing, spreading plant that bears spikes of foamy, white flowers. It is attractive enough to be grown for its foliage alone, and cultivars with interesting variegation are becoming available. This species is native to eastern North America.

T. '**Maple Leaf**' is a clump-forming hybrid with bronze-green, maple-like leaves and pink-flushed flowers.

T. wherryi is similar to *T. cordifolia*, but it forms a clump and bears more flowers. '**Oakleaf**' forms a dense clump of dark green leaves and bears pink flowers.

Problems & Pests

Rust and slugs are possible problems.

'Maple Leaf' (above)

Foxglove
Digitalis

Height: 2–5' **Spread:** 12–24" **Flower color:** pink, purple, yellow, maroon, red, white **Blooms:** late spring, summer **Zones:** 3–8

THESE STARS OF THE ENGLISH COTTAGE GARDEN are biennials or short-lived perennials that are treated as annuals by many Michigan gardeners, and their outstanding performance is worth the expense. I have, however, seen breathtaking stands of these beauties that have re-seeded themselves and persisted for years. Two secrets to success are proper soil preparation and minimal soil disturbance.

Planting

Seeding: Direct sow or start in cold frame in early spring. Seeds need light in order to germinate. Flowering is unlikely the first year.

Planting out: Spring

Spacing: 12–24"

Growing

Foxgloves grow well in **partial or light shade**. The soil should be **fertile, humus rich** and **moist**. Purple Foxglove and Strawberry Foxglove prefer an **acidic** soil, while Yellow Foxglove prefers an **alkaline** soil, but these plants adapt to most soils that are neither too wet nor too dry. Division is unnecessary for Purple Foxglove because this plant will not live long enough to be divided. It continues to occupy your garden by virtue of its ability to self-seed. Yellow Foxglove and Strawberry Foxglove can be divided in spring or fall.

You may wish to deadhead foxgloves once they have finished flowering, but it is a good idea to leave some of the spikes of Purple Foxglove in place to self-seed.

The hybrid varieties become less vigorous with time and self-sown seedlings may not come true to type. Sprinkle new seed in your foxglove bed each spring to ensure a steady show from the lovely flowers.

D. purpurea (this page)

Tips

Foxgloves are must-haves for the cottage garden or for those people interested in heritage plants. They make excellent vertical accents along the back of a border. They also make an interesting addition to a woodland garden. Some staking may be required if the plants are in a windy location. Remove the tallest spike and the side shoots will bloom on shorter stalks that may not need to be staked.

Recommended

D. lutea (Yellow Foxglove, Small Yellow Foxglove) is a true perennial, unlike Purple Foxglove and its cultivars, which are generally biennials. Yellow Foxglove is a clump-forming plant that grows 24" tall and spreads about 12". It bears spikes of yellow flowers in summer.

Foxgloves are extremely poisonous; simply touching one of these plants has been known to cause rashes, headaches and nausea.

D. purpurea 'Alba' (above)

D. x *mertonensis* (Strawberry Foxglove) is also a true perennial. It forms a clump of foliage with flower-bearing stems 3–4' tall. The spring and early-summer flowers are rose pink.

D. purpurea (Purple Foxglove) forms a basal rosette of foliage from which tall flowering spikes emerge, growing 2–5' tall and spreading 24". The flowers bloom in early summer and come in a wide range of colors. The insides of the flowers are often spotted with contrasting colors. If Purple Foxglove is not winter hardy in your garden, it can be grown as an annual from purchased plants. '**Alba**' bears white flowers. '**Apricot**' bears apricot pink flowers. **Excelsior Hybrids,** available in many colors, bear dense spikes of flowers. **Foxy Hybrids,** which also come in a range of colors, are considered dwarf by foxglove standards but easily reach 36" in height.

Problems & Pests

Anthracnose, fungal leaf spot, powdery mildew, root and stem rot, aphids, Japanese beetles and mealybugs are possible problems for foxgloves.

D. purpurea (this page)

The heart medication digitalis is made from extracts of foxglove. For over 200 years, D. purpurea *has been used for treating heart failure.*

Geum
Avens
Geum

Height: 6–24" **Spread:** 8–24" **Flower color:** orange, red, yellow
Blooms: late spring, summer **Zones:** 3–7

IF YOU CAN MAKE GEUMS HAPPY with fast-draining, sandy soil and some late-afternoon shade, they will reward you with masses of bright little blossoms popping out from mounds of green foliage. Deadheading encourages intermittent re-blooming, but geums can't take the heat and often take time out during the dog days of summer. Keep them constantly moist, and you may enjoy an encore of color when the weather cools in late summer.

Planting

Seeding: Direct sow freshly ripened seeds in fall or mid-spring

Planting out: Spring or fall

Spacing: 12–24"

Growing

Geums prefer **full sun** but don't like excessive heat. The soil should be **fertile,** evenly **moist** and **well drained. Alkaline** soil is essential for Creeping Avens. These plants do not like waterlogged soil. Place gravel in the bottom of the planting hole to improve drainage. Geums are semi-evergreen, so wait until spring to cut them back. Divide every year or two in spring or fall to increase their longevity. Cut off spent flowers to keep more coming.

Tips

These plants will make a bright-flowered addition to the border. Creeping Avens works well in rock gardens or raised beds. Geums look particularly attractive when combined with plants that have dark blue or purple flowers.

Recommended

G. coccineum (G. x *borisii)* (Scarlet Avens) forms a mounded clump 12–24" tall, with an equal spread. Scarlet red flowers are borne from late spring to late summer. '**Prince of Orange**' bears bright orange flowers until mid-summer.

G. quellyon (G. chiloense) (Chilean Avens) forms a clump 16–24" tall, with an equal spread. It bears bright scarlet flowers all summer. '**Lady Stratheden**' has bright yellow flowers. '**Mrs. Bradshaw**' bears dark orange semi-double flowers. (Zones 5–7)

G. reptans (Creeping Avens) is a low-growing, trailing plant about 6" tall and 8–12" in spread. Yellow flowers are borne in early summer. (Zones 4–7)

Problems & Pests

Possible problems include downy and powdery mildew, fungal leaf spot, leaf smut and caterpillars.

Species of Geum *grow in mountainous regions worldwide.*

G. quellyon

Globe Thistle
Small Globe Thistle
Echinops

Height: 2–4' **Spread:** 24" **Flower color:** blue, purple
Blooms: late summer **Zones:** 3–8

GLOBE THISTLE'S HANDSOME ROUND FLOWERHEADS and interesting texture make a striking addition to the summer garden. In the center of a border, combine this plant with 'Bicolor' monkshood and Purple Coneflower for an eye-catching mix of colors and patterns. Globe Thistle is long-lived, but the spiny leaves can be a real pain in moving or dividing the plant, so place it in a permanent position. Early deadheading will increase the number of blooms. You will be happy to see more blooms, because they make excellent cut flowers that can be used in both fresh and dried arrangements.

Planting

Seeding: Direct sow in spring

Planting out: Spring or fall

Spacing: 18–24"

This plant is a good choice for gardeners who need a large, low-maintenance specimen to fill an unused corner.

Growing

Globe Thistle prefers **full sun** but tolerates partial shade. The soil should be of **poor to average fertility** and **well drained**. Divide in spring when the clump appears dense or overgrown and begins to show less vigorous or dead areas. Wear gloves and long sleeves to protect yourself from the prickles.

Deadheading prevents self-seeding. Cutting back to the basal foliage after flowering may result in a second round of blooms.

Tips

Globe Thistle is a striking plant for the back or center of the border and for neglected areas of the garden that often miss watering.

Recommended

E. ritro forms a compact clump of spiny foliage. It bears round clusters of purple or blue flowers in late summer. **'Vietch's Blue'** has smaller but more abundant flowers.

Problems & Pests

Globe Thistle rarely has any problems, but aphids can show up from time to time.

Goat's Beard
Aruncus

Height: 6"–6' **Spread:** 1–6' **Flower color:** cream, white
Blooms: early summer, mid-summer **Zones:** 3–7

THESE SHOWY PERENNIALS are covered with masses of frothy, astilbe-like plumes for four weeks in early summer. Because of the size of Common Goat's Beard, it should be treated as a shrub and is best used in areas of the garden where it will have lots of room. Dividing an older stand of this plant can be a challenge. Some books suggest using a knife, but gardeners in the field say a sharp axe or even a chain saw is a more appropriate tool. It's best to plant your goat's beard where it won't need to be disturbed once established.

Planting

Seeding: Use fresh seed and keep soil moist and conditions humid. Soil temperature should be 70–75° F.

Planting out: Spring or fall

Spacing: 18"–6'

Growing

These plants prefer **partial to full shade.** If planted in deep shade, they bear fewer blooms. They also tolerate full sun as long as the soil is kept evenly moist. The soil should be **rich** and **moist,** with plenty of **humus** mixed in. Divide in spring or fall, though goat's beard plants may be

difficult to divide because they often develop a thick root mass. Use a sharp knife to cut the root mass into pieces.

Goat's beards tend to self-seed, but deadheading maintains an attractive appearance and encourages a longer blooming period. If you want to start some new plants from seed, allow the seedheads to ripen before removing them. You will need to have both male and female plants in order to produce seeds that will sprout. Don't save male flower-heads—they will not produce seeds.

Tips

These plants look very natural growing at the sunny entrance or edge of a woodland garden, in a native plant garden or in a large island planting. They may also be used in a border or alongside a stream or pond.

Recommended

A. aethusifolius (Dwarf Korean Goat's Beard) forms a low-growing, compact mound. It grows 6–16" tall and spreads up to 12". Branched spikes of loosely held, cream flowers appear in early summer. This plant looks similar to astilbe and is some-times sold by that name.

A. dioicus (Common Goat's Beard, Giant Goat's Beard) forms a large, bushy, shrub-like perennial 3–6' tall, with an equal spread. Large plumes of creamy white flowers are borne from early to mid-summer. There are several cultivars, though some can be hard to find. **Var.** *astilbioides* is a dwarf variety that grows only 24" tall. **'Kneiffii'** is a dainty cultivar with finely divided leaves and arch-ing stems with nodding plumes. It grows about 36" tall and spreads 18".

'Zweiweltkind' ('Child of Two Worlds') is a compact plant with drooping, white flowers.

Male goat's beard plants have full, fuzzy flowers; female plants have more pendulous flowers.

Problems & Pests

Occasional problems with fly larvae and tarnished plant bugs are possible.

Golden Marguerite
Marguerite Daisy
Anthemis

Height: 8–36" **Spread:** 24–36" **Flower color:** yellow, orange, cream, white
Blooms: summer **Zones:** 3–7

ANY GARDEN WILL LIGHT UP in summer with masses of daisy-like golden marguerites in shades of yellow, cream or white. Mix yellow and white varieties with the blues of salvias or speedwells for a winning combination. The yellow blooms of 'Kelwayi' make particularly lovely cut flowers. Shear golden marguerites back to the basal growth in August to prevent excessive re-seeding and to allow the plants to get ready for winter. In spring, clean up tatty leaves in preparation for the summer show.

Planting

Seeding: Direct sow in spring

Planting out: Spring

Spacing: 18–24"

Growing

Golden marguerites prefer to grow in **full sun**. The soil should be of **average fertility** and **well drained**. These plants are drought tolerant. The clumps tend to die out in the middle and should be divided every two or three years in spring or fall.

Flowering tends to occur in waves. Cut off the dead flowers to encourage continual flowering all summer. If the plants begins to look thin and spread out, cut them back hard to promote new growth and flowers. These plants are avid self-seeders, so deadhead if you don't want new plants popping up all over.

To avoid the need for staking, cut plants back in May or group several plants together so they can support each other. Otherwise, when the plants are young, insert small, twiggy branches as supports.

Tips

Golden marguerites form attractive clumps that blend wonderfully into a cottage-style garden. Their drought tolerance makes them ideal for rock gardens and exposed slopes.

Recommended

A. marshalliana (Marshall Camomile) is a low, mounding plant up to 18" tall. Its finely divided leaves are covered in long, silvery hairs. Bright golden yellow flowers are borne in summer.

A. tinctoria forms a mounded clump of foliage that is completely covered in bright or pale yellow, daisy-like flowers in summer. **'Beauty of Grallach'** has deep orange-yellow flowers. **'E.C. Buxton'** has flowers with creamy yellow petals and yellow centers. **'Grallach Gold'** has bright golden yellow flowers. **'Kelwayi'** bears rich, yellow flowers, up to 2" in diameter. **'Moonlight'** has large, pale yellow flowers. **'Sauce Hollandaise'** flowers have pale, creamy petals with bright yellow centers.

Problems & Pests

Golden marguerites may occasionally have problems with aphids and with fungal problems such as powdery or downy mildew.

Hardy Geranium
Cranesbill Geranium
Geranium

Height: 4–36" **Spread:** 12–36" **Flower color:** white, red, pink, purple, blue
Blooms: spring, summer, fall **Zones:** 3–8

FOR YEARS THESE PLANTS were overshadowed by their showy cousins, the annual geraniums. Now, finally, the hardy geraniums are coming into their own in perennial gardening circles. The number of hybrids available today is astounding. Long blooming and deer resistant, hardy geraniums are at home edging borders, spilling over rock ledges and threading their way under shrubs and other taller plants as groundcovers.

Planting

Seeding: Species are easy to start from seed in early fall or spring. Cultivars and hybrids may not come true to type.

Planting out: Spring or fall

Spacing: 12–24"

Growing

Hardy geraniums grow well in **full sun, partial shade** or **light shade**. Some tolerate heavier shade. These plants dislike hot weather. Soil of **average fertility** and **good drainage** is preferred, but most conditions are tolerated except water-logged soil. Renard's Geranium needs a poor, well-drained soil to grow well.

Divide in spring. Shear back spent blooms for a second set of flowers. If the foliage looks tatty in late summer, prune it back to rejuvenate.

Tips

These long-flowering plants are great in the border, filling in the spaces between shrubs and other larger plants and keeping the weeds down. They can be included in rock gardens and woodland gardens and mass planted as groundcovers.

Recommended

G. cinereum (Grayleaf Geranium) forms a basal rosette of gray-green foliage. It grows 4–6" tall and spreads about 12". It produces small clusters

G. pratense (above),
G. sanguineum (below)

G. sanguineum (above),
G. x oxonianum (below)

*Hardy geraniums
are often called
cranesbills because
the distinctive seed
capsule resembles
a crane's long bill.*

of white or pink-veined flowers in early summer.
It is often grown in rock gardens and other well-
drained spots. '**Ballerina**' has silvery foliage and
pink flowers darkly veined in purple. (Zones 5–8)

G. '**Johnson's Blue**' forms a spreading mat of
foliage 12–18" tall and about 30" wide. It bears
bright blue flowers over a long period in summer.

G. macrorrhizum (Bigroot Geranium, Scented
Cranesbill) forms a spreading mound of fragrant
foliage. It grows 12–20" tall and spreads 16–24".
This plant is quite drought tolerant. Flowers in
variable shades of pink are borne in spring and
early summer. '**Album**' bears white flowers in
summer on compact plants. '**Bevan's Variety**'
bears magenta flowers.

G. x *oxonianum* is a vigorous, mound-forming
plant with attractive evergreen foliage; it bears
pink flowers from spring to fall. It grows up to
30" tall and spreads about 24". '**A.T. Johnson**'
bears many silvery pink flowers. '**Wargrave Pink**'
is a very vigorous cultivar that grows 24" tall,
spreads about 36" and bears salmon pink flowers.

G. pratense (Meadow Cranesbill) forms an
upright clump, growing 24–36" tall and spreading
about 24". Many white, blue or light purple flowers are borne for a short period in early summer.
It self-seeds freely. '**Mrs. Kendall Clarke**' bears
rose pink flowers with blue-gray veining.
'**Plenum Violaceum**' bears purple double flowers
for a longer period than the species because it sets
no seed.

G. renardii (Renard's Geranium) forms a clump
of velvety, deeply veined, crinkled foliage about
12" tall, with an equal spread. A few purple-
veined white flowers appear over the summer, but
the foliage is the main attraction.

G. sanguineum (Bloody Cranesbill, Bloodred
Cranesbill) forms a dense, mounding clump. It
grows 6–12" tall and spreads 12–24". Bright
magenta flowers are borne mostly in early summer and sporadically until fall. '**Album**' has white
flowers and a more open habit than the other

cultivars. **'Alpenglow'** has bright rosy red flowers and dense foliage. **'Elsbeth'** has light pink flowers with dark pink veins. The foliage turns bright red in fall. **'Shepherd's Warning'** is a dwarf plant to 6" tall with rosy pink flowers. **Var.** *striatum* is heat and drought tolerant. It has pale pink blooms with blood red veins.

Problems & Pests

Rare problems with leaf spot and rust can occur.

G. s. var. *striatum* (above), *G. p.* 'Plenum Violaceum' (below)

Hens and Chicks
Roof Houseleek
Sempervivum

Height: 3–6" **Spread:** 12" to indefinite **Flower color:** red, yellow, white, purple; plant grown mainly for foliage **Blooms:** summer **Zones:** 3–8

WITH THE RENEWED INTEREST IN ROCK GARDENING, hens and chicks are now a hot commodity in the gardening world, and collectors are scouring garden centers for unusual specimens. These drought-hardy members of the stonecrop family are great for making living wreaths and for planting in stone troughs and other shallow containers filled with gravelly soil. Hens and chicks are often found in stone pots in old cottage gardens, seeming to depend on only Mother Nature for care.

Planting
Seeding: Not recommended. Remove and re-plant young rosettes to propagate.

Planting out: Spring

Spacing: 10–12"

Growing

Grow these plants in **full sun** or **partial shade**. The soil should be of **poor to average fertility** and very **well drained**. Add fine gravel or grit to the soil to provide adequate drainage. Once a plant blooms, it dies. When you deadhead the faded flower, pull up the soft parent plant as well to provide space for the new daughter rosettes that sprout up, seemingly by magic. Divide by removing these new rosettes and rooting them.

Tips

These plants make excellent additions to rock gardens and rock walls, where they will even grow right on the rocks.

Recommended

S. tectorum forms a low-growing mat of fleshy-leaved rosettes, each about 6–10" across. Small new rosettes are quickly produced that grow and multiply to fill almost any space. Flowers may be produced in summer but are not as common in colder climates. 'Atropurpureum' has dark reddish purple leaves. 'Limelight' has yellow-green, pink-tipped foliage. 'Pacific Hawk' has dark red leaves that are edged with silvery hairs.

Alternate Species

S. arachnoideum (Cobweb House-leek) is identical to *S. tectorum* except that the tips of the leaves are entwined with hairy fibers, giving the appearance of cobwebs. This plant is hardy to Zone 5 in Michigan and may need protection during wet weather.

Problems & Pests

Hens and chicks are generally pest free, although some problems with rust and root rot can occur.

These plants can grow on almost any surface. In the past they were grown on tile roofs, and it was believed they would protect the house from lightning.

Hollyhock
Alcea

Height: 2–9' **Spread:** 12" **Flower color:** yellow, white, apricot, pink, red, purple, reddish black **Blooms:** summer, fall **Zones:** 3–7

WHEN I WAS A CHILD, Hollyhock was nicknamed 'alley plant' because it thrived in the dry, gravelly soil along back fences and garages. Today, this tough-as-nails plant is a treasured part of English and cottage-style gardens. Children still love to play with the flowers and seedheads, fashioning them into tiny dolls with colorful satin skirts.

Planting

Seeding: Direct sow in fall or start indoors in mid-winter. Flowers should be produced the first summer. Plants started in spring or summer should flower the following summer.

Planting out: Spring or fall

Spacing: 24–36"

The powdered roots of plants in the mallow family, to which Hollyhock belongs, were once used to make a soft lozenge for sore throats. Though popular around the campfire, marshmallows no longer contain the throat-soothing properties they originally did.

Growing

Hollyhock prefers **full sun** but tolerates some shade. The soil should be of **average fertility** and **well drained**. Plant in an area that is sheltered from strong winds. Division is unnecessary for this short-lived perennial. Rotate the planting site each year or two to help keep rust problems at bay.

Many Hollyhock cultivars will self-seed, or you can collect the seeds yourself for planting. To propagate cultivars that don't come true to type from self-sown seed (or to propagate any Hollyhock you enjoy), carefully detach the small daughter plants that develop around the base of the plant and replant them where you want them.

'Nigra' (above)

With one or both of these techniques, you should be able to keep strong, healthy Hollyhock plants coming back year after year in your garden.

Promptly remove leaves peppered with tiny orange dots of rust to help keep the disease under control. In fall, leave healthy basal growth intact but remove and burn any tatty leaves.

Tips

Use Hollyhock as a background plant or in the center of an island bed. A fence or wall will provide shelter and support. Stake plants in a windy location.

Hollyhock plants become shorter and bushier if the main stem is pinched out early in the season, when it is about 6–12" tall. The flowers are smaller, but the plant

is less likely to be broken by wind and can therefore be left unstaked.

Old-fashioned Hollyhock varieties commonly have single flowers and grow very tall. The main advantage to using older varieties is a higher resistance to disease.

Recommended

A. rosea is a short-lived perennial that bears flowers on tall spikes. It reappears in the garden by virtue of being a prolific self-seeder. It grows 3–9' tall and about 12" wide. From mid- or late summer to fall, it bears flowers in shades of yellow, white, pink or purple. **'Chater's Double'** bears ruffled double flowers in many bright and pastel shades. This cultivar grows 6–8' tall and is more consistently perennial than the species.

'**Majorette**' is a popular dwarf cultivar that grows 24–36" tall. The semidouble flowers are in shades of yellow, white, red and apricot. '**Nigra**' bears single flowers in a unique shade of reddish black, with yellow throats. '**Summer Carnival**' is an early-blooming cultivar that features double flowers in a wide range of colors.

Problems & Pests

Hollyhock rust is the worst problem, but Hollyhock can also have trouble with leaf spot, mallow flea beetles, aphids, slugs, Japanese beetles and, when plants are young, cutworms.

Hollyhock was originally grown as a food plant. The leaves were added to salads.

Hosta
Plantain Lily
Hosta

Height: 4–36" **Spread:** 1–4' **Flower color:** white or purple; plant grown mainly for foliage **Blooms:** summer, early fall **Zones:** 3–8

LUSH LEAVES IN AN ALMOST INFINITE ARRAY of shapes, sizes and patterns make hostas the darlings of the shade garden. Leaf colors range from chartreuse and bluish green to combinations of yellow, gold, cream and green. And those bitten by the collector bug will find no shortage of new and interesting introductions to pick from. One of the best loved variegated varieties, 'Gold Standard,' was introduced by the late Pauline Banyai, affectionately known as the Hosta Lady of Royal Oak.

Hosta leaves develop best if the plants are left undivided for many years.

Planting

Seeding: Direct sow or start in cold frame in spring. Young plants can take three or more years to reach flowering size.

Planting out: Spring

Spacing: 1–4'

Growing

Hostas prefer **light or partial shade** but will grow in full shade. Some newer varieties tolerate full sun. Morning sun is preferable to afternoon sun. The soil should be **fertile, moist** and **well drained,** but most soils are tolerated. Hostas are fairly drought tolerant, especially if given a mulch to help retain moisture.

Division is not required but can be done every few years in spring or summer to propagate new plants.

Tips

Hostas make wonderful woodland plants, looking very attractive when combined with ferns and other fine-textured plants. Hostas are also good plants for a mixed border, particularly when used to hide the ugly, leggy lower stems and branches of some shrubs. The dense growth and thick, shade-providing leaves of hostas make them useful for suppressing weeds.

Although hostas are commonly grown as foliage plants, they are becoming more appreciated for

Once established, these hardy plants need little attention. Water them occasionally and keep them mulched with a rich organic layer.

H. fortunei 'Gold Standard'

the spikes of lily-like flowers, some of which are fragrant and make lovely cut flowers. Some gardeners, however, find that the flower color clashes with the leaves, which are the main decorative feature of the plant. If you don't like the look of the flowers, feel free to remove them before they open—this will not harm the plant.

Recommended

Hostas have been subjected to a great deal of crossbreeding and hybridizing, resulting in hundreds of cultivars, many whose exact parentage is uncertain. The cultivars below have been grouped with generally accepted parent species.

H. fortunei (Fortune's Hosta) is the parent of many hybrids and cultivars. It has broad, dark green foliage and bears lavender purple flowers in mid-summer. It quickly becomes a dense clump 12–24" tall and 24–36" wide. 'Albomarginata' has variable cream or white margins on the leaves. 'Aureomarginata' has yellow-margined leaves and is more tolerant of sun than many cultivars. 'Francee' is often listed without a parent species. It has puckered, dark green leaves with a narrow white margin. 'Gold Standard' is also often listed without a species. The bright yellow leaves have a narrow green margin.

H. plantaginea (Fragrant Hosta) has glossy, bright green leaves with distinctive veins; it grows 18–30" tall, spreads to about 36" and bears large, white, fragrant flowers in late summer. 'Aphrodite' has white double flowers. 'Honeybells' has sweetly fragrant, light purple flowers. 'Royal Standard' is a durable, low-growing plant 4–8" tall and up to 36" in spread. The dark green leaves are

deeply veined, and the flowers are light purple.

H. sieboldiana (Siebold's Hosta) forms a large, impressive clump of blue-green foliage. It grows about 36" tall and spreads up to 4'. The early-summer flowers are a light grayish purple that fades to white. **'Blue Angel'** has wavy, blue-green foliage and white flowers. **'Elegans'** (var. *elegans*) has deeply puckered, blue-gray foliage and light purple flowers. It was first introduced to gardens in 1905 and is still popular today. **'Frances Williams'** ('Yellow Edge') has puckered blue-green leaves with yellow-green margins. **'Great Expectations'** has pale yellow or cream leaves with wide, irregular, blue-green margins.

H. sieboldii (Seersucker Hosta) grows 12–30" tall and spreads about 20–24". It has undulating, narrow, green leaves with white margins. In late summer and early fall it bears light purple flowers with darker purple veins inside. **'Alba'** has light green leaves with undulating margins and white flowers. **'Kabitan'** has narrow, bright yellow foliage with undulating green margins. This compact cultivar grows about 8" tall and spreads 12".

Problems & Pests

Slugs, snails, leaf spot, crown rot and chewing insects such as black vine weevils are all possible problems for hostas. Varieties with thick leaves tend to be more slug resistant.

Hostas are considered by some gardeners to be the ultimate in shade plants. They are available in a wide variety of leaf shapes, colors and textures.

H. fortunei 'Francee'

Iris
Iris

Height: 4"–4' **Spread:** 6"–4' **Flower color:** many shades of pink, red, purple, blue, white, brown, yellow **Blooms:** spring, summer, sometimes fall **Zones:** 3–10

THE SHOWY BEARDED IRIS was a staple in my grandmother's garden. That iris, like the Variegated Iris, with its crisp green-and-white-striped leaves, is a high-maintenance plant but worth it—if you have the time. In today's hectic world, though, where the gardening mantra is 'easy to grow,' Siberian Iris might be a better choice. That iris has delicate-looking flowers and grassy foliage; it resists borers and other diseases that plague some of its cousins; and it rarely needs dividing. After flowering, the foliage holds its color through the season and turns gold in fall.

Planting

Seeding: Not recommended; germination is erratic and hybrids and cultivars may not come true to type

Planting out: Late summer or early fall

Spacing: 2"–4'

Growing

Irises prefer **full sun** but tolerate very light or dappled shade. The soil should be **average** to **fertile** and **well drained.** Japanese Iris and Siberian Iris prefer a moist but still well-drained soil.

Divide in late summer or early fall. Bearded Iris and Variegated Iris should be divided yearly. When dividing Bearded Iris rhizomes, re-plant so the flat side of the foliage fan will face out to the garden. Dust the toe-shaped rhizome with a powder cleanser before planting to help prevent soft rot.

The wall of a 3500-year-old Egyptian temple features an iris, making this plant one of the oldest cultivated ornamentals.

I. germanica

Deadhead irises to keep them tidy. Cut the foliage of Siberian Iris back in spring.

Tips

Irises are popular border plants, but Japanese Iris and Siberian Iris are also useful alongside a stream or pond, and dwarf cultivars make attractive additions to rock gardens.

It is a good idea to wash your hands after handling irises because they can cause severe internal irritation if ingested. Make sure they are not planted close to places where children play.

Recommended

I. ensata (*I. kaempferi*) (Japanese Iris) is a water-loving species. It grows up to 36" tall and spreads about 18". White, blue, purple or pink flowers are borne from early to mid-summer. It rarely needs dividing. This species is resistant to iris borers.

I. germanica (Bearded Iris) produces flowers in all colors. This iris has been used as the parent plant for many desirable cultivars. Cultivars may vary in height and width from 6" to 4'. Flowering periods range from mid-spring to mid-summer and some cultivars flower again in fall.

I. pallida (Variegated Iris, Sweet Iris) is rarely grown, but the variegated cultivars are a popular addition to the perennial garden. Light purple flowers are borne on plants that grow about 24" tall and spread 12". 'Aureo-variegata' has gold-and-green-striped foliage. 'Variegata' has cream-and-green-striped leaves.

I. reticulata (Netted Iris) forms a small clump 4–10" tall. This semi-hardy iris bears flowers in various shades of blue and purple. The plants grow from bulbs and can be left undisturbed. Bulbs may divide naturally and plants may not flower

I. sibirica

again until the bulbs mature. (Zones 5–10)

I. sibirica (Siberian Iris) is more resistant to iris borers than other species. It grows 2–4' tall and 36" wide. It flowers in early summer; cultivars are available in many shades, mostly purple, blue and white. Plants take a year or two to recover after dividing.

Problems & Pests

Irises have several problems that can be prevented or mitigated through close observation. Iris borers are a potentially lethal pest. They burrow their way down the leaf until they reach the root, where they continue eating until there is no root left at all. The tunnels they make in the leaves are easy to spot, and if any infected leaves are removed and destroyed or the borers squished within the leaf, the borers will never reach the roots.

Leaf spot is another problem that can be controlled by removing and destroying infected leaves. Be sure to give irises the correct growing conditions. Too much moisture for some species will allow rot diseases to settle in and kill the plants. Plant rhizomes high in the soil to deter root rot. Slugs, snails and aphids may also cause some trouble.

Powdered iris root, called orris, smells like violets when crushed and can be added to perfumes and potpourris as a fixative.

I. germanica

Joe-Pye Weed
Boneset, Snakeroot
Eupatorium

Height: 2–7' **Spread:** 18"–4' **Flower color:** white, purple, blue, pink
Blooms: late summer, fall **Zones:** 3–9

THESE SHOWY MICHIGAN NATIVES are a common sight along many roadsides and borders of wetlands, but don't overlook them when it comes to choosing perennials for your garden. They put on an impressive parade of long-lasting color in late summer and fall. Some species may reach up to 7' or even more in fertile ground. The compact 'Chocolate,' with its striking bronze-purple foliage and white flowers, adds interest to the garden all summer. And talk about contrast: in late summer and fall, this cultivar is covered with masses of sweetly fragrant white flowers. It's a knockout combined with black-eyed Susans and tall grasses.

Planting

Seeding: Start seed indoors in late winter or early spring; soil temperature should be 59–68° F

Planting out: Spring

Spacing: 18–36"

Growing

Joe-Pye weed plants prefer **full sun** but tolerate partial shade. The soil should be **fertile** and **moist**. Wet soils are tolerated. Divide plants in spring when clumps become overgrown. Don't put off dividing if space is a problem, because dividing oversized clumps is a tough job.

It may take a couple of seasons for these plants to mature, so don't crowd them. Pruning growth back in May encourages branching and lower, denser growth, but it can delay flowering.

Tips

These plants can be used in a moist border or near a pond or other water feature. The tall types are ideal in the back of a border or center of a bed where they will create a backdrop for lower-growing plants. *E. coelestinum* might seem a tad weedy for a formal border, but it will make a fantastic addition to a native planting.

Recommended

E. coelestinum (Conoclinium coelestinum) (Hardy Ageratum, Blue Boneset, Mist-flower) is a bushy, upright plant that grows 24–36" tall and spreads 18–36". From late summer until frost it bears clusters of flossy, light blue to lavender flowers. 'Album' bears white flowers.

E. maculatum is a huge plant. It grows 5–7' tall and spreads 3–4'. In late summer it bears clusters of purple flowers. 'Gateway' is slightly shorter, growing up to 6' tall. The large flower clusters are rose pink and the plant's stems are reddish.

E. rugosum (Ageratina altissima) (Boneset, White Snakeroot) forms a bushy, mounding clump of foliage. It grows 3–4' tall, or taller, and spreads 24–36". Clusters of white flowers appear in late summer and early fall. 'Chocolate' grows 2–3' tall and has dark bronzy purple leaves that mature to dark green.

Problems & Pests

These plants may have occasional problems with powdery mildew, fungal leaf spot, rust, aphids, whiteflies and leaf miners.

The flowers attract butterflies to the garden and can be used in fresh arrangements.

E. rugosum 'Chocolate'

Lady's Mantle
Alchemilla

Height: 3–18" **Spread:** 20–24" **Flower color:** yellow, green
Blooms: early summer to early fall **Zones:** 3–7

ACCORDING TO LEGEND, the Virgin Mary wore lady's mantle as an adornment. Lady's mantle plants were also used to make herbal remedies to treat a variety of female complaints. Today the velvet-like, gray-green leaves of these low-mounding beauties add a touch of elegance to any garden. The plants can be used as a continuous border edging or interplanted with flowering annuals such as impatiens. Early in the season, when lady's mantle plants are in bloom, other plants may be overshadowed, but later the foliage forms a rich textural backdrop for other denizens of the garden. In partial shade, lady's mantles may also work as groundcovers.

Poets and alchemists were inspired by the crystal-like dew that collects on the leaves; the dew was reputed to have magical and medicinal qualities.

Planting

Seeding: Direct sow fresh seed or start in containers; transplant while seedlings are small

Planting out: Spring

Spacing: 24"

Growing

Lady's mantle plants prefer **light shade** or **partial shade,** with protection from the afternoon sun. They dislike hot locations, and excessive sun will scorch the leaves. The soil should be **fertile, humus rich, moist,** and **well drained.** These plants are drought resistant once established. Division is rarely required but can be done in spring before flowering starts or in fall once flowering is complete. If more plants are desired, move some of the self-seeded plants, which are bound

A. alpina (above), *A. mollis* (below)

A. mollis (this page)

to show up, to where you want them. Deadhead the spent flowers to keep things looking tidy and prevent excessive re-seeding.

Tips

Lady's mantles are ideal for grouping under trees in woodland gardens and for border edges, where they soften the bright colors of other plants. A wonderful location is alongside a pathway that winds through a lightly wooded area.

If your lady's mantle begins to look tired and heat stressed during summer, rejuvenate it in one of two ways. Trim the whole plant back, encouraging new foliage to fill in, or remove the dead leaves and then trim the plant back once the new foliage has started to fill in. Leave plants intact over the winter, then clean them up in spring.

Recommended

A. alpina (Alpine Lady's Mantle) is a diminutive, low-growing plant that grows 3–5" tall and spreads up to 20". Soft white hairs on the backs of the leaves give the appearance of a silvery margin around each leaf. Clusters of tiny, yellow flowers are borne in summer.

A. mollis (Common Lady's Mantle) is the most frequently grown species. It grows 8–18" tall and spreads up to about 24". Plants form a mound of soft, rounded foliage, above which are held sprays of frothy-looking, yellowish green flowers in early summer. Deadheading may encourage a second flush of flowers in late summer or fall.

Problems & Pests

Lady's mantles rarely suffer from any problems, though fungi may be troublesome during warm, wet summers. These plants are deer resistant.

The airy flowers make a fabulous filler for fresh and dried flower arrangements, and the leaves can be boiled to make a green dye for wool.

A. mollis

Lamb's Ears
Woolly Betony
Stachys

Height: 6–18" **Spread:** 18–24" **Flower color:** pink, purple; plant also grown for foliage **Blooms:** summer **Zones:** 3–8

CHILDREN DELIGHT in petting this lovely plant's furry, silver leaves, which indeed look and feel like the ears of a lamb. *Stachys* (*sta*-kis) is a favorite for edging in herb gardens and borders, but as a season-long performer it gets mixed reviews. After a fantastic show of foliage in spring, the plants tend to go into a bit of decline, especially if the weather is wet for any length of time. Early deadheading helps to minimize that decline, but removing dead leaves in summer is usually necessary. 'Big Ears' is not quite as showy but is less susceptible to summer decline.

Planting
Seeding: Direct sow or start in containers in cold frame in spring

Planting out: Spring

Spacing: 18–24"

Cut flowerheads when they are in bud or after they bloom, and hang them to dry for use in dried flower arrangements.

Growing

Lamb's Ears grows best in **full sun**. The soil should be of **poor or average fertility** and **well drained**. Leaves can rot in humid weather if the soil is poorly drained. Divide in spring.

Remove spent flower spikes to keep plants looking neat. Select a flower-less cultivar if you don't want to deadhead. Cut back diseased or damaged foliage; new foliage will sprout when the weather cools.

Tips

Lamb's Ears makes a great ground-cover in a new garden where the soil has not yet been amended. It can be used to edge borders and pathways, providing a soft, silvery backdrop for more vibrant colors in the border.

Leaves can look tatty by the middle of summer. The more of this plant you use, the more you will have to clean up. Plant only as much as you will tend, or plant in an out-of-the-way spot where the stressed foliage will not be as noticeable.

Recommended

S. byzantina (S. lanata) forms a mat of thick, woolly rosettes of leaves. Pinkish purple flowers are borne all summer. **'Big Ears'** ('Helen von Stein') has greenish silver leaves that are twice as big as those of the species. **'Silver Carpet'** has silvery white, fuzzy foliage; it rarely, if ever, produces flowers.

Problems & Pests

Fungal leaf problems including rot, powdery mildew, rust and leaf spot are rare but can occur in hot, humid weather.

Lavender
English Lavender
Lavandula

Height: 8–36" **Spread:** up to 4' **Flower color:** purple, pink, blue
Blooms: mid-summer to fall **Zones:** 5–9

IF YOU HAVE EVER SEEN the fields of Lavender in the south of France, you know what magic this plant can create in the garden. Fast-draining, sandy soil and full sun are two keys to hardiness. Gardening books will tell you it must not be cut back hard, but I have whacked mine back to 4" when it suffered heavy winter kill, and it came roaring back. The secret is to wait until the green buds of new growth begin to show before pruning in spring. The variety 'Munstead' has a good reputation for winter hardiness in Michigan. Plant extra so that you can enjoy the scented blossoms in the garden and in dried arrangements too.

Planting

Seeding: Start in fall or spring in a cold frame; plants don't always come true to type

Planting out: Spring

Spacing: 12–24"

Growing

Lavender grows best in **full sun.** The soil should be **average to fertile** and **alkaline,** and it must be **well drained.** Once established, this plant is heat and drought tolerant. It is woody and cannot be divided, but 3–4" cuttings can be taken in early spring. The cuttings can be started in damp sand and each should have a heel attached. (A heel cutting has a small strip of woody growth at the base.)

Deadhead to encourage a second bloom. Growth can be trimmed back in spring and late summer. Never cut into old woody growth as Lavender does not form new shoots from old wood. Frequent trimming keeps plants from becoming too woody. Allow new buds to emerge

L. angustifolia 'Hidcote' (above),
L. angustifolia (below)

L. angustifolia 'Jean Davis' (above)

in spring before cutting to show you how far back you can cut. Always leave at least one of these new buds in place when cutting a branch back. Avoid heavy pruning after August to give plants time to harden off before winter.

In colder areas, Lavender should be covered with mulch and, if possible, a good layer of snow. Gardeners in cold areas may have to replace plants every few years if too much growth is killed back in winter.

Tips

Lavender is a wonderful, aromatic edging plant and can be used as a low hedge. Good companions for this deer-resistant plant include other drought-tolerant specimens, such as pinks, thymes, Lamb's Ears, sedums and Goldenrod.

To dry the flowers, cut them when they show full color but before the flowers open completely.

Recommended

L. angustifolia is an aromatic, bushy shrub that is often treated as a perennial. It grows up to 36" tall and spreads up to 4'. From mid-summer to fall, it bears spikes of small flowers in varied shades of purple. **'Hidcote'** ('Hidcote Blue') bears spikes of deep purple flowers and grows 18–24" tall. **'Jean Davis'** is a compact cultivar with spikes of pale pink flowers. It grows 12–14" tall. **'Lady'** can be grown from seed and will flower the first summer. It grows 8–10" tall and bears purple flowers. **'Munstead'** is a compact plant that grows to about 18" and spreads up to 24". Its flowers are lavender blue.

Problems & Pests

As is the case with many aromatic plants, the pest problems are few. Keep an eye open for root rot and fungal leaf spot, particularly during wet summers, when the soil may stay wet for extended periods.

The scent of Lavender is considered to be relaxing and soothing and is often used in aromatherapy. Dry a few sprigs for use in scented sachets and pillows or in the bath.

Ligularia
Ligularia

Height: 3–6' **Spread:** 2–5' **Flower color:** yellow, orange; plant also grown for foliage **Blooms:** summer, sometimes early fall **Zones:** 4–8

SHADE GARDENERS LOOKING FOR PLANTS to provide dramatic foliage with strong vertical accents will love ligularias. From mid- to late summer these tall plants covered with large, heart-shaped leaves produce shooting spires of yellow flowers that create an exciting look. However, the sight of a stressed ligularia wilting in the heat of the afternoon sun is not pretty, so be careful when positioning. The dramatic, toothed foliage will contrast nicely in texture and color with any of the variegated hostas.

Planting

Seeding: Species can be started outdoors in spring in containers; cultivars rarely come true to type

Planting out: Spring

Spacing: 2–5'

Growing

Ligularias should be grown in **light shade** or **partial shade** with protection from the afternoon sun. The soil should be of **average fertility**, **humus rich** and consistently **moist**. Division is rarely, if ever, required but can be done in spring or fall to propagate a desirable cultivar.

Tips

Use ligularias alongside a pond or stream. They can also be used in a well-watered border or naturalized in a moist meadow or woodland garden.

L. stenocephala 'The Rocket' (above), *L. dentata* (below)

The leaves can wilt in hot sun, even in moist soil. They will revive at night, but this won't help how horrible they look during the day. If your ligularia looks wilted, it is best to move the plant to a cooler, more shaded position in the garden.

Recommended

L. dentata (Bigleaf Ligularia, Golden Groundsel) forms a clump of rounded, heart-shaped leaves. It grows 3–5' tall and spreads 3–4'. In summer and early fall it bears clusters of orange-yellow flowers, held above the foliage. **'Desdemona'** and **'Othello'** are two similar cultivars. They have orange flowers and purple-green foliage. They come fairly true to type when grown from seed.

L. przewalskii (Shevalski's Ligularia) also forms a clump but has deeply incised leaves. It grows 4–6' tall and spreads 2–4'. In mid- and late summer it produces yellow flowers on long purple spikes.

L. dentata (above),
L. s. 'The Rocket' (below)

L. stenocephala (Narrow-spiked Ligularia) has toothed rather than incised foliage and bears bright yellow flowers on dark purple-green spikes. It grows 3–5' in height and width. This species is closely related to the previous one, and **'The Rocket'** may be a hybrid of the two. This cultivar has heart-shaped leaves with ragged-toothed margins. The dark leaf veins become purple at the leaf base.

Problems & Pests

Ligularias have no serious problems, though slugs can damage young foliage.

L. dentata (above),
L. stenocephala (below)

Lungwort
Pulmonaria

Height: 8–24" **Spread:** 8–36" **Flower color:** blue, red, pink, white, purple; plant also grown for foliage **Blooms:** spring **Zones:** 3–8

WITH A NAME LIKE LUNGWORT, you have to be good looking to make it in the green world—and these fabulous plants are just that. Handsome foliage combined with delightful pink, blue or white spring flowers makes these plants highly prized for the shade garden. The more common varieties, such as 'Mrs. Moon,' have been upstaged by newcomers such as 'Spilled Milk' and 'Berries and Cream,' spurring plant collectors to search for new patterns of speckled and splotched leaves.

Planting

Seeding: Start seed in containers outdoors in spring; plants don't consistently come true to type

Planting out: Spring or fall

Spacing: 12–18"

Growing

Lungworts prefer **partial to full shade**. The soil should be **fertile, humus rich, moist** and **well drained**. Rot can occur in very wet soil. Lungworts are hardy throughout Michigan.

Divide in early summer after flowering or in fall. Provide the newly planted divisions with lots of water to help them re-establish. Shear plants back lightly after flowering to deadhead and show off the fabulous foliage, and to keep the plants tidy.

Tips

Lungworts make useful and attractive groundcovers for shady borders, woodland gardens and edges of ponds and streams.

P. longifolia (above), *P. saccharata* (below)

These plants have more than 20 common names. Many are biblical references, such as Abraham, Isaac and Jacob, Adam and Eve, Children of Israel and Virgin Mary.

P. saccharata (above), *P. longifolia* (below)

Recommended

P. angustifolia (Blue Lungwort) forms a mounded clump of foliage. The leaves have no spots. This plant grows 8–12" tall and spreads 18–24". Clusters of bright blue flowers, held above the foliage, are borne from early to late spring.

P. longifolia (Long-leaved Lungwort) forms a dense clump of long, narrow, white-spotted, green leaves. It grows 8–12" tall and spreads 8–24". It bears clusters of blue flowers in spring or even earlier, as the foliage emerges.

P. officinalis (Common Lungwort, Spotted Dog) forms a loose clump of evergreen foliage, spotted with white. It grows 10–12" tall and spreads about 18". Spring flowers

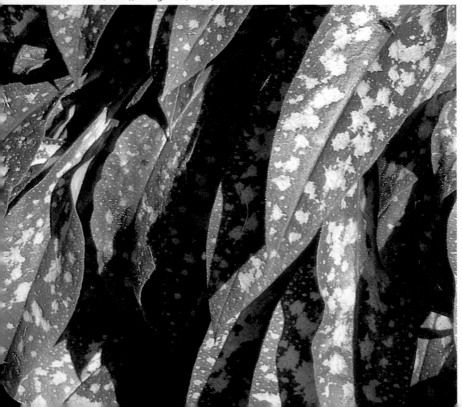

open pink and mature to blue. This species was once grown for its reputed medicinal properties, but it is now valued for its ornamental qualities. '**Cambridge Blue**' bears many blue flowers. '**Sissinghurst White**' has pink buds that open to white flowers. The leaves are heavily spotted with white.

P. rubra (Red Lungwort) forms a loose clump of unspotted, softly hairy leaves. It grows 12–24" tall and spreads 24–36". Bright red flowers appear in early spring. '**Redstart**' has pinkish red flowers.

P. saccharata (Bethlehem Sage) forms a compact clump of large, white-spotted, evergreen leaves. It grows 12–18" tall, with a spread of about 24". The spring flowers may be purple, red or white. This species has given rise to many cultivars and hybrids. '**Berries and Cream**' has foliage heavily spotted with silver and bears raspberry red flowers. '**Janet Fisk**' is very heavily spotted and appears almost silvery in the garden. Its pink flowers mature to blue. '**Mrs. Moon**' has pink buds that open to a light purple-blue. The leaves are dappled with silvery white spots. '**Pink Dawn**' has dark pink flowers that age to purple. '**Spilled Milk**' is a compact plant with silvery green splotched leaves and pink flowers.

Problems & Pests

Lungworts may become susceptible to powdery mildew if the soil dries out for extended periods. Remove and destroy damaged leaves. These plants are generally problem free.

Pulmonaria *species (usually* P. officinalis) *are traditional culinary and medicinal herbs. The young leaves may be added to soups and stews to flavor and thicken the broth. When dried, the spotted leaves also make an attractive addition to potpourri.*

P. saccharata

Lychnis
Maltese Cross, Rose Campion
Lychnis

Height: 2–4' **Spread:** 12–18" **Flower color:** magenta, white, scarlet, red, orange **Blooms:** summer **Zones:** 3–8

IF BRIGHT FUCHSIA TURNS YOUR CRANK, then *Lychnis* (*lik*-nis) species are the plants for you. Tuck them in the center of the border in bunches and mix them with tall pink soapworts, 'David' phlox and Russian Sage. Rose Campion *(L. coronaria)* has 1" blooms that shoot up from silver gray, felted basal foliage, filling the garden with colorful confetti. For those who favor softer colors, 'Angel's Blush' produces white flowers with a delicate pink blush. Another lychnis, Maltese Cross, bears tennis ball–sized clusters of bright red, white or orange flowers on stiff upright stems from early to mid-summer.

Planting

Seeding: Start seeds in late spring; soil temperature should be 68–70° F

Planting out: Spring

Spacing: 12–18"

Growing

Lychnis plants grow well in **full sun** but enjoy some afternoon shade to protect them from excessive heat. The soil should be of **average fertility and well drained**. These plants do not tolerate heavy soils; if you garden in clay, use raised beds or backfill the planting space with soil mixed with chicken grit or gravel. Division can be done in spring, though lychnis plants may not live long enough to need it.

Although these plants are short-lived and should almost be treated as annuals or biennials, in light or gravelly soils they re seed prolifically. Basal cuttings can also be taken to propagate the plants.

Tips

Lychnis plants make beautiful, care-free additions to a border, cottage garden or naturalized garden.

These tall plants may need some support, particularly in a windy location. Peony supports or twiggy branches pushed into the soil are best and are less noticeable than having the plants tied to stakes.

Recommended

L. chalcedonica (Maltese Cross) is a stiff, upright plant growing 3–4' tall and 12–18" wide. The scarlet flowers are borne in clusters from early to mid-summer. Some support may be

required to keep this plant standing upright. 'Alba' has white flowers.

L. coronaria (Rose Campion) forms an upright mass of silvery gray leaves and branching stems. It grows 24–36" tall and about 18" wide. In late summer the plant is dotted with magenta pink flowers, which are very striking against the silvery foliage. 'Alba' has white flowers. 'Angel's Blush' bears white flowers that have reddish pink centers. 'Atrosanguinea' has red flowers.

L. chalcedonica (above), *L. coronaria* (below)

Mallow
Malva

Height: 8"–4' **Spread:** 12–24" **Flower color:** purple, pink, white, blue
Blooms: summer, fall **Zones:** 4–9

MALLOWS ARE STAPLES in the classic cottage garden. Give them full sun and well-drained soil and these easy-to-grow, drought-tolerant workhorses will thrive or, as some put it, grow like weeds. Red shrub roses, Feverfew and white or blue Peach-leaved Bellflower make nice companions. An old southern favorite and a smaller hollyhock look-alike, the dainty 'Zebrina' is one of my favorites. This short-lived perennial is a snap to grow from seed, so save some seed in case your plant fails to return the following season. Cut back old flower stems to 8–10" when the blooming slows to thwart excessive re-seeding and encourage a second flush of flowers.

Some mallows are called 'cheese' or 'cheese plant' because the round, flattened fruits resemble wheels of cheese.

Planting

Seeding: Direct sow indoors or out in spring or early summer

Planting out: Spring, summer

Spacing: 12–24"

Growing

Mallows grow well in **full sun** or **partial shade**. The soil should be of **average fertility, moist** and **well drained**. These plants are drought tolerant. In rich soils they may require staking. Mallows do not need dividing. Propagate by basal cuttings taken in spring.

Mallows readily self-seed. Cutting plants back by about half in late May will encourage more compact, bushy growth but will delay flowering by a couple of weeks. Transplant or thin out seedlings if they are too crowded.

M. sylvestris 'Zebrina' (above),
M. alcea 'Fastigiata' (below)

Some types of mallow are reputed to have a calming effect when ingested and were used in the Middle Ages as antidotes for aphrodisiacs and love potions.

Tips

Use mallows in a mixed border or in a wildflower or cottage garden. Dead-head to keep the plants blooming until October. Mallows also make good cut flowers.

Recommended

M. alcea (Hollyhock Mallow) is a loose, upright, branching plant. It grows 2–4' tall, spreads 18–24" and bears pink flowers with notched petals all summer. '**Fastigiata**' has a neat, upright form. If deadheaded, it continues to produce flowers well into fall.

M. moschata (Musk Mallow) is a bushy, upright plant with musk-scented leaves. It grows about 36" tall, spreads about 24" and bears pale pink or white flowers all summer. '**Pirouette**' ('Alba') bears pure white flowers.

M. sylvestris 'Primley Blue' (this page)

M. sylvestris (Cheeses) may be upright or spreading in habit. Plants of this species grow 8"–4' tall and spread 12–24". The pink flowers have darker veins and are produced all summer. Many cultivars are available. '**Bibor Felho**' features an upright form and rose purple blooms with darker purple veins. '**Braveheart**,' also an upright cultivar, has light purple-pink flowers with dark purple veins. '**Primley Blue**' has light purple-blue flowers. This is a prostrate cultivar, growing only about 8" tall. '**Zebrina**' has pale pink or white flowers with purple veins and is an upright grower.

Problems & Pests

Problems with rust, leaf spot, Japanese beetles and spider mites can occur occasionally.

M. sylvestris 'Bibor Felho' (above),
M. moschata (below)

Meadow Rue
Thalictrum

Height: 2–5' **Spread:** 12–36" **Flower color:** pink, purple, yellow, white
Blooms: summer, fall **Zones:** 3–8

IT IS SURPRISING that, with a winning combination of fern-like leaves and fluffy clouds of flowers, meadow rues are not more common in our mixed borders and cottage gardens. But these plants have yet to hit the big time in Michigan. With half a dozen species that offer plants ranging in height from 9" to 6', there is something here for every garden. These deer-resistant beauties thrive in moist woodland gardens and partially shaded borders where summer color is hard to come by. If your garden has areas like these, give one of the meadow rues a whirl.

Planting

Seeding: Direct sow in fall or start indoors in early spring; soil temperature should be 70° F

Planting out: Spring

Spacing: 12–24"

Growing

Meadow rues prefer **light or partial shade** but tolerate full sun if the soil remains moist. The soil should be **humus rich, moist** and **well drained.** These plants rarely need to be divided. If necessary for propagation, divide in spring as the foliage begins to develop. Plants may take a while to re-establish once they have been divided or have had their roots disturbed.

Tips

In the middle or at the back of a border, meadow rues make a soft backdrop for bolder plants and flowers and are beautiful when naturalized in an open woodland or meadow garden.

T. r. 'Lavender Mist' (above), T. aquilegifolium (below)

Meadow rue flowers are generally petalless. The unique flowers consist of showy sepals and stamens.

These plants often do not emerge until quite late in spring. Mark the location where they are planted so that you do not inadvertently disturb the roots if you are cultivating their bed before they begin to grow.

Do not place individual plants too close together because their stems can become tangled.

Recommended

T. aquilegifolium (Columbine Meadow Rue) forms an upright mound 24–36" tall, with an equal spread. Pink or white plumes of flowers are borne in early summer. The leaves are similar in appearance to those of columbines. '**Thundercloud**' ('Purple Cloud') has dark purple flowers. '**White Cloud**' has white flowers.

T. delvayi
'Hewitt's Double' (this page)

T. delvayi (Yunnan Meadow Rue) forms a clump of narrow stems that usually need staking. It grows 4–5' tall and spreads about 24". It bears fluffy purple or white flowers from mid-summer to fall. **'Album'** bears white flowers. **'Hewitt's Double'** is a popular cultivar that produces many tiny, purple, pompom-like flowers.

T. rochebruneanum **'Lavender Mist'** (Lavender Mist Meadow Rue) forms a narrow, upright clump. It grows 3–5' tall and spreads 12–24". The late-summer blooms are lavender purple and have numerous distinctive yellow stamens.

Problems & Pests
Infrequent problems with powdery mildew, rust, smut and leaf spot can occur.

T. r. 'Lavender Mist' (above),
T aquilegifolium (below)

Meadowsweet

Filipendula

Height: 2–8' **Spread:** 18"–4' **Flower color:** white, cream, pink, red
Blooms: late spring, summer, fall **Zones:** 3–8

WITH NAMES LIKE QUEEN-OF-THE-PRAIRIE and Queen-of-the-
Meadow, you might suspect that these plants are not shy performers. Deep
green leaves that hold their lush form make these plants valuable foliage
specimens from spring through frost. But the big show comes in summer,
when the tall stems are covered with eye-catching pink or white, fluffy
flowerheads. Though they look like queens, you won't have to cater to these
lovelies to keep them happy. All they ask is moist soil and a good supply of
sun and they will put on a regal performance for a decade or more. Dropwort, a species with a slightly less elegant name, reaches only 24" in height
and is a good choice for smaller gardens.

Planting

Seeding: Germination can be erratic; start seed in cold frame in fall and keep soil evenly moist

Planting out: Spring

Spacing: 18–36"

Growing

Meadowsweet plants prefer **partial or light shade**. Full sun is tolerated if the soil remains sufficiently moist. The soil should be **fertile, deep, humus rich** and **moist**. Divide in spring or fall. You may need a sharp knife to divide these plants, as they grow thick, tough roots. Meadowsweets tend to self-seed, and if dividing them seems daunting to you, transplanting the seedlings could be an easier way to get new plants. These plants can be deadheaded if desired, but the faded seedheads are quite attractive when left in place.

The flowers of F. ulmaria were often used to flavor ales and mead in medieval times, giving rise to the name meadowsweet, from the Anglo-Saxon word medesweete.

F. rubra

F. *ulmaria* (above), F. *rubra* (below)

Tips

Most meadowsweets are excellent plants for bog gardens or wet sites. Grow them alongside streams or in moist meadows. Meadowsweets may also be grown in the back of a border, as long as they are kept well watered.

F. vulgaris prefers dry soil. It is a good choice if you can't provide the moisture the other species need.

The flowers of *F. ulmaria*, once used to flavor mead and ale, are now becoming popular as a flavoring for vinegars and jams. They may also be made into a pleasant wine, which is made in much the same way as dandelion wine.

Recommended

F. purpurea (Japanese Meadowsweet) forms a clump of stems and large, deeply lobed foliage. It grows up to 4' tall and spreads about 24". Pinkish red flowers fade to pink in late summer. **'Elegans'** has fragrant white flowers. The spent flowerheads develop an attractive red tint.

F. rubra (Queen-of-the-Prairie) forms a large, spreading clump 6–8' tall and 4' in spread. It bears clusters of fragrant, pink flowers from early to mid-summer. **'Venusta'** bears very showy pink flowers that fade to light pink in fall.

F. ulmaria (Meadowsweet, Queen-of-the-Meadow) bears cream white flowers in large clusters. It grows to be 24–36" tall and 24" wide. **'Aurea'** has yellow foliage that matures to light green as summer progresses. **'Flore Pleno'** has double flowers.

F. vulgaris (Dropwort, Meadowsweet) is a low-growing species up to 24" tall and 18" wide. **'Flore Pleno'** has white double flowers, and **'Rosea'** has pink flowers.

Problems & Pests

Powdery mildew, rust and leaf spot can be troublesome.

In the 16th century it was customary to strew rushes and herbs to insulate the floor underfoot, freshen the air and combat infections. Meadowsweet was the herb Queen Elizabeth I preferred for these purposes.

F. ulmaria

Monkshood
Aconitum

Height: 3–6' **Spread:** 12–18" **Flower color:** purple, blue, white
Blooms: mid- to late summer **Zones:** 3–8

FOR PEOPLE WHO HAVE A PASSION for blue flowers, monkshoods are a late-season treasure. They are also just the thing for those gardeners who find delphiniums too challenging. Pair these violet blue standouts with *Sedum* 'Autumn Joy' and *Anemone* 'Honorine Jobert.' Once established, monkshood plants have staying power and don't appreciate moving, so plan the site carefully and then sit back and enjoy. All parts of these pretty plants are poisonous, so if small children share your patch, pass on planting monkshood until they grow up.

Aconitum *may come from the Greek* akoniton, *meaning 'dart.' The ancient Chinese and the Arabs used the juice of monkshood to poison arrow tips.*

Planting

Seeding: Germination may be irregular. Seeds direct sown in spring may bloom the following summer; seeds sown later will not likely bloom for yet another year.

Planting out: Spring; bare-rooted tubers may be planted in fall

Spacing: 18"

A. x cammarum 'Bicolor' (above),
A. napellus (below)

Growing

Monkshoods prefer to grow in **light or partial shade** but tolerate sun if the climate is cool. These plants will grow in any **moist** soil but prefer to be in a **rich** soil with lots of **organic matter** worked in.

Monkshoods prefer not to be divided, as they may be a bit slow to re-establish. If division is desired to increase the number of plants, it should be done in late fall or early spring. When dividing or transplanting monkshoods, the crown of the plant should never be planted at a depth lower than where it was previously growing. Burying the crown any deeper will cause it to rot and the plant to die.

Tall monkshoods may need to be staked. Peony hoops or tomato cages inserted around young plants will be hidden as the plants fill in.

Tips

Monkshood plants are perfect for cool, boggy locations along streams or next to ponds. They make tall, elegant additions to a woodland garden in combination with lower-growing plants. Avoid planting monkshoods near the roots of trees

A. *napellus* (above),
A. x *cammarum* 'Bicolor' (below)

because these plants cannot compete with trees.

Monkshoods prefer conditions to be on the cool side. They will do poorly when the weather gets hot, particularly if conditions do not cool down at night. Mulch the roots to keep them cool.

Recommended

A. x *cammarum* (Cammarum Hybrids) is a group of hybrids that contains several of the more popular cultivars. '**Bicolor**' (Bicolor Monkshood) bears blue and white flowers. The flower spikes are often branched. '**Bressingham Spire**' bears dark purple-blue flowers on strong spikes. It grows up to 36" tall but needs no staking.

A. charmichaelii (Azure Monkshood) forms a low mound of basal leaves from which the flower spikes emerge. The foliage generally grows

to about 24" in height, but the plant can grow to 6' tall when in flower. Purple or blue flowers are borne a week or so later than those of other species. **'Arendsii'** bears dark blue flowers on strong spikes that need no staking.

A. napellus (Common Monkshood) is an erect plant that forms a basal mound of finely divided foliage. It grows 3–5' tall, spreads 12–18" and bears dark purple-blue flowers.

A. napellus (this page)

Problems & Pests

Problems with aphids, root rot, stem rot, powdery mildew, downy mildew, wilt and rust can occur.

Always take care to avoid getting the juice from monkshood plants in open wounds or in your mouth or eyes.

Obedient Plant
False Dragonhead
Physostegia

Height: 1–4' **Spread:** 12–24" **Flower color:** pink, purple, white
Blooms: mid-summer to fall **Zones:** 2–9

THESE DEPENDABLE PLANTS stand up well to the tough end-of-season weather conditions. But some gardeners suggest their common name be changed to *dis*obedient plant because of their invasive habit. Dividing every year or two will keep the beast under control. For an outstanding combination, mix a white or pink variety with *Caryopteris*, Russian Sage and Purple Coneflower. Hummingbirds love to sip from the tiny, snapdragon-like flowers, so place your obedient plant where you can watch the show.

Planting

Seeding: Direct sow in early fall or in spring with soil temperature 70–75° F. Protect fall-started seedlings from winter cold the first year.

Planting out: Spring or fall

Spacing: 12–24"

The individual flowers can be bent around on the stems and will stay put where you leave them. It is this unusual habit that gives the plant its common name.

Growing

Obedient plants prefer **full sun** but tolerate partial or light shade. The soil should be **moist** and of **average to high fertility**. In a fertile soil these plants are more vigorous and may need staking. Choose a compact cultivar to avoid the need for staking. Plants can become invasive. Divide in early to mid-spring, once ground can be worked, every two years or so to curtail invasiveness.

Tips

Use these plants in borders, cottage gardens, informal borders and naturalistic gardens. The flowers of obedient plants can be cut for use in fresh arrangements.

Recommended

P. virginiana has a spreading root system from which upright stems sprout. It grows 2–4' tall and spreads 24" or more. **'Crown of Snow'** ('Snow Crown') has white flowers. **'Pink Bouquet'** bears bright pink flowers. **'Summer Snow'** is a more compact, less invasive plant with white flowers. **'Variegata'** is a desirable variegated specimen with cream-margined leaves and bright pink flowers.

P. **'Vivid'** bears bright purple-pink flowers. This compact hybrid grows 12–24" tall and 12" wide.

Problems & Pests

Rare problems with rust and slugs are possible.

'Variegata' (above),
P. virginiana (below)

Oriental Poppy
Papaver

Height: 18"–4' **Spread:** 18–36" **Flower color:** red, orange, pink, white
Blooms: spring, early summer **Zones:** 3–7

IT'S HARD TO SAY WHICH HAS DONE MORE to make poppies famous:
the bright red Veteran's Day blossom or the intoxicating field of poppies in
The Wizard of Oz. The secret to success in growing the vibrant perennial
Oriental Poppy is loose, fast-draining soil. The plant goes dormant after it
flowers, but fresh foliage appears in late summer or early autumn, so when
the leaves wither don't think your plant has died and dig it up. Leave the seedheads in place to encourage re-seeding and to attract finches to the garden.

Planting
Seeding: Direct sow in spring or fall

Planting out: Spring

Spacing: 24"

Growing

Grow Oriental Poppy in **full sun**. The soil should be **average to fertile** and must be **well drained**. Division is rarely required but may be done in fall once new rosettes begin to form. Plants die back after flowering and send up fresh new growth in late summer, which should be left in place for winter insulation.

Tips

Small groups of Oriental Poppy look attractive in an early-summer border, although they may leave a bare spot during the dormant period in summer. Baby's breath and catmints make good companions and will fill in any blank spaces.

Recommended

P. orientale forms an upright, oval clump 18"–4' tall and 24–36" wide. Red, scarlet, pink or white flowers with prominent black stamens are borne in late spring and early summer. '**Allegro**' has bright scarlet red flowers. '**Carneum**' bears salmon pink flowers. '**Pizzicato**' is a dwarf cultivar, with flowers in a wide range of colors. It forms a mound 18–24" tall, with an equal spread.

Problems & Pests

Problems with powdery mildew, leaf smut, gray mold, root rot and damping off are possible but rare in well-drained soil.

Use of poppy seeds in cooking and baking can be traced as far back as the ancient Egyptians.

Penstemon
Beard Tongue
Penstemon

Height: 9"–5' **Spread:** 6–24" **Flower color:** white, yellow, pink, purple, red
Blooms: late spring, summer, fall **Zones:** 4–8

PENSTEMONS PUT ON A WONDERFUL SHOW of color in late spring or early summer, and some long bloomers continue on. While many cultivars are listed as hardy to Zone 4, the drought-tolerant penstemons demand dry, sunny locations with sandy, fast-draining soil and are therefore often only marginally hardy in Michigan gardens, where clay soil abounds. I'm experimenting with penstemons in raised beds, heavily amended with compost, builder's sand and soil conditioner.

Planting

Seeding: Start indoors in late summer or early spring; soil temperature should be 55–64° F

Planting out: Spring or fall

Spacing: 12–24"

Growing

Penstemons prefer **full sun** but tolerate some shade. The soil should be of **average to rich fertility, sandy** and **well drained**. These plants are drought tolerant and will rot in wet soil. Mulch in winter with chicken grit or pea gravel to protect the crowns from exposure to excessive moisture and cold.

Divide every two to three years in spring. Pinch plants when they are 12" tall to encourage bushy growth.

Tips

Use penstemons in a herbaceous or mixed border, a cottage garden or a rock garden.

Twiggy branches pushed into the ground around young plants will support them as they grow.

Recommended

P. 'Alice Hindley' bears pinkish purple flowers with white throats from mid-summer to fall. It grows 24–36" tall and spreads 12–18".

P. 'White Bedder'

P. 'Apple Blossom' bears pink-flushed white flowers from late spring to mid-summer. This rounded perennial grows 18–24" tall, with an equal spread.

P. barbatus is an upright, rounded perennial. It grows 18–36" tall and spreads 12–18". Red or pink flowers are borne from early summer to early fall. 'Alba' has white flowers. 'Elfin Pink' is very reliable and has compact spikes of pink flowers. It grows up to 18" tall. 'Hyacinth Mix' is a hardy seed strain producing a mix of pink, lilac, blue and scarlet flowers on plants up to 12" tall. 'Praecox Nanus' ('Nanus Rondo') is a compact, dwarf plant about half the size of the species. It bears pink, purple or red flowers. 'Prairie Dusk' bears tall spikes of tube-shaped, rose purple flowers over a long season. *P. barbatus* and its varieties are the hardiest of the penstemons.

P. digitalis (Foxglove Penstemon) is a very hardy, upright, semi-evergreen perennial. It grows 2–5' tall and spreads 18–24". It bears white flowers, often veined with purple, all summer. '**Husker Red**' combines white flowers with vibrant burgundy foliage that adds season-long interest and makes an attractive mass planting. Chosen as the 1996 Perennial Plant of the Year by the American Perennial Plant Association, it was developed for hardiness as well as good looks.

P. '**White Bedder**' grows 24–30" tall and 18" wide. Its white flowers become pink tinged as they mature. It blooms from mid-summer to mid-autumn.

Problems & Pests

Powdery mildew, rust and leaf spot can occur but are rarely serious problems.

Over 200 species of Penstemon *are native to varied habitats from mountains to open plains throughout North and South America.*

Peony
Paeonia

Height: 24–32" **Spread:** 24–32" **Flower color:** white, yellow, pink, red, purple
Blooms: spring, early summer **Zones:** 2–7

MY FIRST GARDENING EXPERIENCE, at the ripe old age of four, took place in the backyard of a neighbor whom I affectionately called 'my friend Mrs. Higgins.' It was a cool day in May and after watering the garden we began cutting huge bouquets of pink and red peonies the size of small cabbages. These old-fashioned plants with their over-the-top blooms are experiencing a resurgence in popularity today. For a fabulous show that runs from mid-May through mid-June, try combining varieties that bloom at different times and have a mix of single, semi-double and double blossoms.

Planting

Seeding: Not recommended; seeds may take two to three years to germinate and many more years to grow to flowering size

Planting out: Fall or spring

Spacing: 24–36"

Growing

Peonies prefer **full sun** but tolerate some shade. The planting site should be well prepared before the plants are introduced. Peonies like **fertile, humus-rich, moist, well-drained** soil, to which lots of compost has been added. Too much fertilizer, particularly nitrogen, causes floppy growth and retards blooming. Division is not required, but it is usually the best way to propagate new plants and it should be done in fall.

Cut back the flowers after blooming and remove any blackened leaves to prevent the spread of gray mold. Red peonies are more susceptible to disease.

In the past, peonies were used to cure a variety of ailments. They are named after Paion, the physician to the Greek gods.

Whether you choose to clean your perennial garden in fall or spring, it is essential to deal with peonies in fall. To reduce the possibility of disease, clean up and discard or destroy all leaf litter before the snow falls.

Tips

These wonderful plants look great in a border when combined with other early-flowering plants. They may be underplanted with bulbs and other plants that will die down by mid-summer, when the emerging foliage of peonies will hide the dying foliage of spring plants. Avoid planting peonies under trees where they will have to compete for moisture and nutrients.

Planting depth is a very important factor in determining whether or not a peony will flower. Tubers planted too shallowly or, more commonly, too deeply will not flower. The buds or eyes on the tuber should be 1–2" below the soil surface.

Place wire peony or tomato cages around the plants in early spring to support heavy flowers. The cage will be hidden by the foliage as it grows up into the wires.

young peony growth (above)

Recommended

Peonies may be listed as cultivars of a certain species or as interspecies hybrids. Hundreds are available.

P. lactiflora (Common Garden Peony, Chinese Peony) forms a clump of red-tinged stems and dark green foliage. It grows up to 30" tall, with an equal spread, and bears fragrant, single, white or pink flowers with yellow stamens. Some popular hybrid cultivars are '**Dawn Pink**' with single, rose pink flowers; '**Duchesse de Nemours**' with fragrant, white double flowers tinged yellow at the bases of the inner petals; and '**Sara Bernhardt**' with large, fragrant, pink double flowers. These cultivars may also be sold as hybrids and not as cultivars of this species.

P. officinalis (Common Peony) forms a clump of slightly hairy stems and deeply lobed foliage. It bears red or pink single flowers with yellow stamens. '**Alba Plena**' has white double flowers. '**Rubra Plena**' has red double flowers.

Problems & Pests

Peonies may have trouble with *Verticillium* wilt, ringspot virus, tip blight, stem rot, gray mold, leaf blotch, nematodes and Japanese beetles.

Peonies are slow growers and often take a couple of years to bloom, but once established they may well outlive their owners. Despite their exotic appearance, these tough perennials can survive winter temperatures as low as −40° F.

Phlox

Phlox

Height: 2"–4' **Spread:** 12–36" **Flower color:** white, orange, red, blue, purple, pink **Blooms:** spring, summer, fall **Zones:** 3–8

IF YOU AREN'T GROWING A PHLOX in your garden, you're missing out on a wonderful show. Moss Phlox creates spectacular carpets of bright blue, pink and white that cover rockeries and walls in spring. Many gardeners avoid growing the taller varieties because they are vulnerable to powdery mildew. Choose disease-resistant varieties, and for later blooms, try 'David,' 'Eva Cullum,' 'Miss Lingard' or 'Rosalinde.' With tall, short, spring-blooming, creeping and other types of phlox, you have much to choose from.

Planting

Seeding: Not recommended

Planting out: Spring

Spacing: 12–36"

The name Phlox *is from the Greek word for 'flame,' referring to the colorful flowers of many species.*

Growing

Garden Phlox and Early Phlox prefer **full sun,** Moss Phlox prefers **partial shade** and *P.* 'Chatahoochee' prefers **light shade.** Creeping Phlox prefers **light to partial shade** but tolerates heavy shade. All like **fertile, humus-rich, moist, well-drained** soil.

Divide in fall or spring. Creeping Phlox spreads out horizontally as it grows. The stems grow roots where they touch the ground. These plants are easily propagated by detaching the rooted stems in spring or early fall. Do not prune Creeping Phlox in fall—it is an early-season bloomer and will have next spring's flowers already forming.

Tips

Low-growing species are useful in a rock garden or at the front of a border. Taller species may be used in the middle of a border, where they are particularly effective if planted in groups.

Garden Phlox requires good air circulation to help prevent mildew. Thin out large stands to help keep the air flowing. Early Phlox is more resistant to powdery mildew than Garden Phlox.

Recommended

P. **'Chatahoochee'** is a low, bushy plant. It grows 6–12" tall and spreads about 12". It produces lavender blue flowers with darker

P. maculata (above), *P. subulata* (below)

purple centers for most of the summer and early fall.

P. maculata (Early Phlox, Wild Sweet William) forms an upright clump of hairy stems and narrow leaves that are sometimes spotted with red. It grows 24–36" tall and spreads 18–24". Pink, purple or white flowers are borne in conical clusters in the first half of summer. This species has good resistance to powdery mildew. **'Miss Lingard'** bears white flowers all summer. **'Omega'** bears white flowers with light pink centers. **'Rosalinde'** bears dark pink flowers. These cultivars are taller than the species, usually 30" or more.

P. paniculata (Garden Phlox) blooms in summer and fall. It has many cultivars, which vary greatly in size, growing 20"–4' tall and spreading 24–36". Many colors are available, often with contrasting centers.

P. paniculata 'David' (above), *P. paniculata* (below)

'Bright Eyes' bears light pink flowers with deeper pink centers. 'David' bears white flowers and is resistant to powdery mildew. 'Eva Cullum' bears pink flowers with red centers. 'Starfire' bears crimson red flowers.

P. stolonifera (Creeping Phlox) is a low, spreading plant. It grows 4–6" tall, spreads about 12" and bears flowers in shades of purple in spring. This species is a former Perennial Plant of the Year.

P. subulata (Moss Phlox, Creeping Phlox, Moss Pinks) is very low growing, only 2–6" tall, with a spread of 20". Its cultivars bloom in various colors from late spring to early summer. 'Candy Stripe' bears bicolored pink and white flowers.

Problems & Pests

Occasional problems with powdery mildew, stem canker, rust, leaf spot, leaf miners and caterpillars are possible.

P. paniculata 'Eva Cullum' (above),
P. subulata 'Candy Stripe' (below)

Phloxes come in many forms, from low-growing creepers to tall, clump-forming uprights. The many species can be found in diverse climates including dry, exposed mountainsides and moist, sheltered woodlands.

Pincushion Flower
Scabiosa

Height: 12–24" **Spread:** 24" **Flower color:** purple, blue, white, pink
Blooms: summer, fall **Zones:** 3–7

WITH ITS MOUNDS OF DARK GREEN FOLIAGE and profusion of lacy, lavender blue flowers that look like large buttons on a fancy dress, *Scabiosa* 'Butterfly Blue' is a winner. It was selected as Perennial Plant of the Year in 2000 by both the American Perennial Plant Association and the Michigan Nursery and Landscape Association. Whether used at the front of a border or as a small-scale groundcover, this tough little cookie will continue to bloom all summer if kept deadheaded. Those who enjoy pink may want to try 'Pink Mist.' Once established, this plant is winter hardy if planted in very well-drained soil.

Planting

Seeding: Direct sow in spring or summer

Planting out: Spring

Spacing: 24"

Growing

Pincushion flowers prefer **full sun** but tolerate partial shade. The soil should be **light, moderately fertile, neutral** or **alkaline** and **well drained**. Divide in early spring, whenever the clumps become overgrown.

Remove the flowers as they fade to promote a longer flowering period. Cutting flowers at their peak every few days for indoor use will make this maintenance chore more enjoyable. Leave the evergreen foliage intact over the winter and remove dead and tattered leaves in spring.

Tips

Pincushion flowers look best planted in groups of three or more in a bed or border. They are also used as cut flowers.

Recommended

S. caucasica forms a basal rosette of narrow leaves. Blue or lavender flowers are borne in summer on long stems that grow up to 24" tall; the plant spreads 24" as well. 'Fama' bears sky blue flowers with silvery white centers. 'House's Hybrids' (Isaac House Hybrids) is a group of slightly smaller plants with large, shaggy blue flowers. 'Miss Wilmont' bears white flowers.

Several hybrids have been developed from crosses between *S. caucasica* and *S. columbaria*, a smaller species. These hybrids may be listed as cultivars of either species. 'Butterfly Blue' bears lavender blue flowers from early summer until frost. 'Pink Mist' grows about 12" tall and bears many pink blooms from summer to frost.

Problems & Pests

Pincushion flowers rarely have problems, though aphids may be troublesome.

S. caucasica (this page)

Pinks

Dianthus

Height: 2–18" **Spread:** 8–24" **Flower color:** pink, red, white, lilac
Blooms: spring, summer **Zones:** 3–9

PINKS WERE FIRST PROPAGATED in the 16th century and are frequently referred to as Gillyflower in the works of William Shakespeare. With 80 species of the genus to choose from, it's not surprising that these easy-to-grow, colorful charmers with their clove-like fragrance have lasted through the gardens of time. Their ability to thrive in alkaline soil makes them great choices for most Michigan gardens when excellent drainage is provided.

Planting

Seeding: Not recommended; cultivars do not come true to type from seed

Planting out: Spring

Spacing: 10–20"

Growing

Pinks prefer **full sun** but tolerate some light shade. A **well-drained, neutral** or **alkaline** soil is required. The most important factor in successful cultivation of pinks is drainage—they dislike standing in water. Mix sharp sand or gravel into their area of the flowerbed to encourage good drainage.

Pinks may be difficult to propagate by division. It is often easier to take cuttings in summer, once flowering has finished. Cuttings should be 1–3" long. Strip the lower leaves from the cutting. The cuttings should be kept humid, but be sure to give them some ventilation so that fungal problems do not set in.

The lovely, delicate petals of pinks can be used to decorate cakes. Be sure to remove the white part at the base of the petal before using the petals or they will be bitter.

D. deltoides (below)

Tips

Pinks make excellent plants for rock gardens and rock walls, and for edging flower borders and walkways. They can also be used in cutting gardens and even as groundcovers.

Deadhead as the flowers fade to prolong blooming, but leave a few flowers in place to go to seed. Pinks self-seed quite easily. Seedlings may differ from the parents, often with interesting results.

Recommended

D. x *allwoodii* (Allwood Pinks) forms a compact mound and bears flowers in a wide range of colors. Cultivars generally grow 8–18" tall, with an equal spread. **'Doris'** bears semi-double, salmon pink flowers with darker pink centers. It is popular as a cut flower. **'Laced Romeo'** bears spice-scented red flowers with cream-margined petals. **'Sweet Wivelsfield'** bears fragrant, two-toned flowers in a variety of colors.

D. deltoides (Maiden Pink) grows 6–12" tall and about 12" wide. The plant forms a mat of foliage and flowers in spring. This is a popular species to use in rock gardens. **'Brilliant'** ('Brilliancy,' 'Brilliance') bears dark red flowers. **'Zing Rose'** bears carmine red blooms.

D. gratianopolitamus (Cheddar Pink) usually grows about 6" tall but can grow up to 12" tall and 18–24" wide. This plant is long-lived and forms a very dense mat of evergreen, silver gray foliage with sweet-scented flowers borne in summer. '**Bath's Pink**' bears plentiful, light pink flowers and tolerates warm, humid conditions. '**Petite**' is an even smaller plant than the species, growing 2–4" tall, with pink flowers.

D. plumarius (Cottage Pink) is noteworthy for its role in the development of many popular cultivars known as Garden Pinks. They are generally 12–18" tall and 24" wide, although smaller cultivars are available. They all flower in spring and into summer if deadheaded regularly. The flowers can be single, semi-double or fully double and are available in many colors. '**Sonata**' bears fragrant double flowers in many colors all summer. '**Spring Beauty**' bears double flowers in many colors with more strongly frilled edges than the species.

Problems & Pests

Providing good drainage and air circulation will keep most fungal problems at bay. Occasional problems with slugs, blister beetles, sow bugs and grasshoppers are possible.

D. plumarius (this page)

Cheddar Pink is a rare and protected species in Britain. It was discovered in the 18th century by British botanist Samuel Brewer, and it became as locally famous as Cheddar cheese.

Plume Poppy
Macleaya

Height: 6–10' **Spread:** 12–36"; clumps spread indefinitely
Flower color: cream **Blooms:** mid- to late summer **Zones:** 3–10

PLUME POPPY IS THE GENTLE GIANT of the perennial
world, soaring up to 10' in height. The large, palm-shaped
leaves of light green with silver undersides wave gently in
the breeze, and in summer the plant is topped with fluffy,
white, 12" plumes of flowers. Because this plant is so large,
it looks best from a distance, and the invasive nature of its
root system means Plume Poppy should be reserved for
spaces that can handle a large crowd.

Planting

Seeding: Start seed in
cold frame in early or
mid-spring

Planting out: Spring

Spacing: 36"

Growing

Plume Poppy prefers **full sun** but tolerates partial shade. The soil should be of **average fertility, humus rich** and **moist**. Plume Poppy tolerates dry soils and is less invasive in poorer conditions. Divide every two or three years to control the size of the clump.

Remove spent flowers if you want to avoid having too many self-sown seedlings popping up all over the garden. Pull up or cut back any overly exuberant growth as needed. Planting in a heavy-duty, bottom-less pot sunk into the ground will slow invasive spreading.

Tips

Plume Poppy looks impressive as a specimen plant or at the back of the border. Be sure to give it lots of room, because it can quickly over-whelm less vigorous plants.

Drought-tolerant and easy to care for, Plume Poppy makes a nice sum-mer screen and is also a good choice for the centers of cement-bordered medians and large island beds.

Recommended

M. cordata is a tall, narrow, clump-forming plant with attractive, undu-lating, lobed leaves and plumes of creamy white flowers. Each clump spreads 12–36", but clumps of plants may spread indefinitely.

Problems & Pests

Slugs may attack young growth. Anthracnose can be a problem in warm, humid weather.

The flower plumes of these unusual members of the poppy family add a dramatic flair to fresh or dried arrangements.

Primrose
Primula

Height: 6–24" **Spread:** 6–18" **Flower color:** red, orange, pink, purple, blue, white, yellow **Blooms:** spring, early summer **Zones:** 3–8

MAKING THEIR DEBUT WITH A CAST OF SPRING BULBS, primroses take center stage in the shade garden. The bright clusters of little flowers are a delight to behold, so plant these beauties at the edge of the border where they will be displayed to full advantage. For a new twist try Chinese Pagoda Primrose, with its dense spikes of tiny lilac flowers topped by scarlet red buds. It will put on a spectacular show in early summer, when color may have faded in the shade garden.

Planting

Seeding: Direct sow ripe seeds at any time of year; start indoors in early spring or in cold frame in fall or late winter

Planting out: Spring

Spacing: 6–18"

Growing

Choose a location for these plants with **light or partial shade**. The soil should be **moderately fertile, humus rich, moist, well drained** and **neutral** or **slightly acidic**. Primroses are not drought resistant and will quickly wilt and fade if they are not watered regularly. Overgrown clumps should be divided after flowering or in early fall. Pull off yellowing or dried leaves in fall for fresh new growth in spring.

Tips

Primroses work well in many areas of the garden. Try them in a woodland area or under the shade of taller shrubs and perennials in a border or rock garden. Moisture-loving primroses may be grown in a bog garden or almost any other moist spot.

The species with flowers on tall stems look lovely when planted in masses, while the species that have

P. japonica (below)

solitary flowers peeking out from the foliage are interesting dotted in odd spots throughout the garden.

Recommended

P. auricula (Auricula Primrose) forms a rosette of smooth, waxy foliage. Large flowers are clustered at the tops of stout stems. The plant grows up to 8" tall and spreads 10". The flowers are usually yellow or cream, but there are many cultivars with flowers in many colors.

P. denticulata (Drumstick Primula, Himalayan Primrose) forms a rosette of spoon-shaped leaves that are powdery and white on the undersides. The plant grows 12–18" tall and spreads 10–12". The flowers, which may be purple, white, pink or red and usually have yellow centers, are borne in dense, ball-like clusters atop thick stems.

P. eliator (Oxslip) is a meadowland species from Europe. It grows about 12" tall and 6" wide. The yellow, tubular flowers are clustered at the ends of long stems.

P. japonica (Japanese Primrose) grows 12–24" tall and 12–18" wide. It thrives in moist, boggy conditions and does poorly if not provided with enough moisture. It is a candelabra flowering type, meaning that the long flower stem has up to six evenly spaced rings of flowers along its length.

P. x polyanthus (Polyantha Primrose, Polyantha Hybrids) usually grows 8–12" tall, with about an equal spread. The flowers are clustered at the tops of stems of variable height. It is available in a wide range of solid colors or bicolors and is often sold as a flowering potted plant.

P. veris (Cowslip Primrose) forms a rosette of deeply veined, crinkled foliage. Small clusters of tubular yellow flowers are borne at the tops of narrow stems. The plant grows

about 10" tall, with an equal spread. The leaves and flowers can be eaten and the flowers used to make wine.

P. vialii (Chinese Pagoda Primrose) forms a rosette of deeply veined leaves. The flowers are borne in small spikes. The spike has a two-toned appearance as the red buds open to reveal light violet flowers, starting with the lowest flowers. The plant grows 12–24" tall and spreads about 12".

P. vulgaris (English Primrose, Common Primrose) grows 6–8" tall and 8" wide. The flowers are solitary and borne at the ends of short stems that grow slightly longer than the leaves.

Problems & Pests

Slugs, strawberry root weevils, aphids, rust and leaf spot are all possible problems for primroses.

P. vialii (above)

Purple Coneflower
Coneflower, Echinacea
Echinacea

Height: 2–5' **Spread:** 12–24" **Flower color:** purple, pink or white, with rust orange centers **Blooms:** mid-summer to fall **Zones:** 3–8

EVEN WITH SCORCHING HEAT, summer drought and hardpan clay, Purple Coneflower thrives in my mixed border. The huge, deep pink, daisy-like flowers last and last, and when Jack Frost arrives, the striking black seedheads are left behind to star in the winter show. Pinching the growth in June will delay blooming and shorten the plants, so if you grow Purple Coneflower in drifts you can orchestrate the bloom time as well as the height. Partner this plant with other North American natives, such as Blazing Star and black-eyed Susans, and give them a backdrop of fluffy blue Russian Sage.

Planting

Seeding: Direct sow in spring

Planting out: Spring

Spacing: 18"

Growing

Purple Coneflower grows well in **full sun** or very **light shade**. Any **well-drained** soil is tolerated, though an **average to rich** soil is preferred. The thick taproot makes this plant drought resistant, but it prefers to have regular water. Divide every four years or so in spring or fall. Deadhead early in the season to prolong flowering. Later you may wish to leave the flowerheads in place to self-seed. If you don't want to allow self-seeding, remove all the flowerheads as they fade. Pinch plants back in early summer to encourage bushy growth that is less prone to mildew.

Tips

Use Purple Coneflower in meadow gardens and informal borders, either in groups or as single specimens. The dry flowerheads make an interesting feature in fall and winter gardens.

Recommended

E. purpurea is an upright plant 5' in height and up to 18" in spread, with prickly hairs all over. It bears purple flowers with orangy centers. The cultivars are generally about half the species' height. **'Magnus'** bears flowers like those of the species but larger, to 7" across. **'White Lustre'** bears white flowers with orange centers. **'White Swan'** is a compact plant with white flowers.

Problems & Pests

Powdery mildew is the biggest problem. Also possible are leaf miners, bacterial spot and gray mold. Vine weevils may attack the roots.

'Magnus' (above),
'Magnus' with 'White Swan' (below)

Echinacea *was an important traditional medicine for Native Americans, and today it is a popular immunity booster in herbal medicine.*

Red-Hot Poker
Torch Lily
Kniphofia

Height: 2–6' **Spread:** about 24" **Flower color:** red, orange, yellow, white
Blooms: summer, fall **Zones:** 5–9

IF YOU'RE LOOKING FOR VIBRANT COLOR and architectural interest, include a stand of red-hot pokers in your summer garden. The bottlebrush-shaped spikes of tubular flowers in bold shades of red, orange and yellow stand out like glowing embers when combined with *Rudbeckia* 'Goldsturm' and a red-flowered lychnis. 'Flamenco,' a new and improved red-hot poker cultivar, was an All-American Winner for 1999.

Planting

Seeding: Not recommended; cultivars do not come true and seedlings may take three years to reach flowering size

Planting out: Spring

Spacing: 24"

Growing

These plants grow best in **full sun**. The soil should be **fertile, humus rich, sandy, moist** and very **well drained**. Large clumps may be divided in late spring. To encourage the plants to continue flowering as long as possible, cut the spent flowers off right where the stem meets the plant.

Red-hot pokers are sensitive to cold weather. Bundle up the leaves in fall and tie them above the center bud to keep the crown protected over the winter. Do not cut back the foliage in fall—it provides winter protection.

Tips

Red-hot pokers make a bold, vertical statement in the middle or back of a border. These plants look best when planted in groups.

Recommended

K. '**Little Maid**' grows to only 24" tall and has salmon-colored buds opening to white flowers.

K. '**Royal Standard**' is a large plant, sometimes growing over 36" tall. Scarlet buds open to bright yellow flowers in late summer.

K. uvaria forms a large clump of long, narrow foliage. It grows 4' tall and spreads about half this much. In fall, bright red buds open to orange flowers that fade to yellow as they age. '**Flamenco**' bears many spikes of white, yellow, orange and red flowers. It grows about 30" tall and spreads about 24". It is reputed to flower the first summer when grown from seed. '**Nobilis**' is a large cultivar. It grows up to 6' tall with long, orange-red flower spikes, borne from mid-summer to fall.

Problems & Pests

These plants rarely have problems but are susceptible to stem or crown rot. Thrips may cause flowers to drop off unopened.

Red-hot pokers are short-lived, so keep the color coming by adding a few new plants every year.

Rockcress
Wall Rockcress
Arabis

Height: 2–12" **Spread:** 12–18" **Flower color:** white, pink
Blooms: spring, early summer **Zones:** 4–7

ROCKCRESSES HERALD THE BEGINNING of the growing season, with bright white sheets of flowers that cascade from rock walls and rock gardens in April. They make sturdy companions for naturalized bulbs, such as grape hyacinths, daffodils and tulips, hiding their fading foliage as the summer wears on. Taking the time to shear rockcress plants back after flowering keeps them from looking somewhat leafless and bedraggled by mid-summer.

Planting

Seeding: Start in containers in early spring; seeds need light to germinate

Planting out: Any time during growing season

Spacing: 12"

Growing

Rockcresses prefer **full sun**. The soil should be of **average or poor fertility, alkaline** and **well drained**. These plants do best in a climate that doesn't have extremely hot summer weather. Divide in early fall every two or three years. Stem cuttings taken from new growth may be started in summer.

Cut the plants back by up to half after flowering to keep them neat and compact and to encourage a possible second flush of blooms. Before winter tidy them up but do not cut them back. Remove dead leaves and tatty growth in spring.

Tips

Use rockcresses in a rock garden, in a border or on a rock wall. They may also be used as groundcovers on an exposed slope or as companion plants with small bulbs. Don't plant rockcresses where they may overwhelm slower-growing plants.

P. procurrens 'Variegata' (below)

Recommended

A. caucasica forms a low mound of small rosettes of foliage. White flowers are borne in early spring. '**Compinkie**' has pink flowers. '**Snow Cap**' ('Schneehaube') produces abundant white flowers.

A. procurrens (*A. ferdinandi-coburgi*) forms a low mat of foliage with small white flowers in spring and early summer. This species is more shade tolerant than *A. caucasica*. '**Variegata**' (Variegated Rockcress) has white-edged foliage.

Problems & Pests

White rust and downy mildew are possible problems. Aphids are occasionally troublesome, along with *Arabis* midge, which causes deformed shoots that should be removed and destroyed.

Species of the genus Arabis *resemble those of* Aubrieta. *Both are commonly known as rockcress, so make sure you write down the scientific name of the plant you want before you head to the garden center.*

Rodgersia
Rodger's Flower, Rodger's Plant
Rodgersia

Height: 2–6' **Spread:** 2–5' **Flower color:** white, pink
Blooms: late spring, summer **Zones:** 5–7

AFICIONADOS OF LARGE LEAVES who need to fill a big space next to a water feature will quickly fall in love with the horsechestnut-like foliage of rodgersias. Like many big-leaved plants, these species need consistent moisture to look their best through the summer. Large clusters of creamy white or pink flowers, reminiscent of astilbe blossoms, rise above the leaves for several weeks in summer. In partial-sun locations, the foliage of Bronzeleaf Rodgersia takes on a bronze cast from mid-summer through autumn.

Planting

Seeding: Start seed indoors in late winter or early spring

Planting out: Spring

Spacing: 24–36"

Growing

Rodgersias grow well in **partial or light shade**. Excessive exposure will cause leaf scorch, so a location that provides protection from winds and hot afternoon sun is best. The soil should be **fertile, humus rich** and **moist**. These plants don't like to dry out, but they tolerate a drier soil in a shaded location. They rarely need dividing, but you can divide them in spring if you want more plants.

Tips

These bold plants give a dramatic and exotic appearance to the garden. They thrive in light shade near a pond or other water feature and can be grown in the back of a border or as specimen plants if they are kept well watered.

Recommended

R. aesculifolia (Fingerleaf Rodgersia) forms a clump of horsechestnut-like leaves. It produces clusters of tiny, white or pink flowers on tall stalks in mid- or late summer.

R. podophylla (Bronzeleaf Rodgersia) has leaves similar to those of Fingerleaf Rodgersia, but it differs in that the foliage takes on a bronzy purple cast in mid-summer and fall. This species bears creamy white flowers from late spring to mid-summer.

Problems & Pests

Rarely, slugs or snails may attack young foliage.

The plumes of flowers can be cut for use in dried arrangements.

R. aesculifolia (this page)

Rose Mallow
Hardy Hibiscus
Hibiscus

Height: 18"–8' **Spread:** 36" **Flower color:** white, red, pink
Blooms: mid-summer to frost **Zones:** 4–9

GARDENERS WHO ENJOY IN-YOUR-FACE COLOR go gaga over Rose Mallow. After all, it's hard to ignore a plant that presents you with big, bright, 6–8" flowers at eye level. Although Rose Mallow requires moist soil conditions, good winter drainage is key to its ability to overwinter. When you purchase a plant, look for named cultivars to be sure you are purchasing a hardy variety. The glowing pink 'Lady Baltimore,' the dashing red 'Lord Baltimore' and the white, pink or red 'Southern Belle' and 'Disco' are all good choices.

Planting

Seeding: Soak seeds, then sow indoors or out in spring. Ensure soil temperature is 55–64° F.

Planting out: Spring

Spacing: 36"

Growing

Grow Rose Mallow in **full sun**. The soil should be **humus rich and moist**. Rose Mallow is a heavy feeder and benefits from a side dressing of fertilizer when it begins to leaf out. Divide in spring.

Prune back by one-half in June for bushier, more compact growth. Deadhead to keep the plant tidy. If you cut your Rose Mallow back in fall, be sure to mark its location because this plant is slow to emerge in spring.

Tips

This is an interesting plant for the back of an informal border or mixed into a pond-side planting. The large flowers create a bold focal point in late-summer gardens.

Recommended

H. moscheutos is a large, vigorous plant with strong stems. It grows 3–8' tall and spreads about 36". The huge flowers can be up to 12" across. **'Blue River II'** grows about 4' tall. It bears pure white flowers. **'Disco'** ('Disco Belle') is a small plant 18–24" tall. It is often grown as an annual, and its flowers can be red, pink or white. **'Lady Baltimore'** bears pink flowers. **'Lord Baltimore'** bears red flowers. **'Southern Belle'** bears red, pink or white flowers on large plants 4–6' tall.

Problems & Pests

Rose Mallow may develop problems with rust, fungal leaf spot, bacterial blight, *Verticillium* wilt, viruses and stem or root rot. A few possible insect pests are whiteflies, aphids, scale insects, mites and caterpillars.

The moisture-loving Rose Mallow is one of the most exotic-looking plants you can include in a bog garden or pond-side planting.

Russian Sage
Perovskia

Height: 3–4' **Spread:** 3–4' **Flower color:** blue, purple
Blooms: mid- or late summer to fall **Zones:** 4–9

IN THE LATE-SUMMER GARDEN, you can't go wrong with a combination of silver foliage and lavender blue flowers. That's why Russian Sage has become an essential in many perennial beds and cottage borders and was selected as the 1995 Perennial Plant of the Year by the American Perennial Plant Association. Give it full sun and fast-draining soil and this deer-resistant, drought-tolerant, low-maintenance beauty will work magic with bold golds, vibrant pinks and beautiful bronzes. 'Filagran' and 'Longin' have all the virtues of the species but bear more delicate foliage and develop a more upright habit.

Planting

Seeding: Not recommended; germination can be very erratic

Planting out: Spring

Spacing: 36"

The flowers make a nice addition to fresh and dried flower arrangements.

Growing

Russian Sage prefers a location with **full sun**. The soil should be **poor to moderately fertile** and **well drained**. Too much water and nitrogen will cause the growth to flop, so take care when growing this plant next to heavy feeders. Russian Sage does not need dividing.

In spring, when new growth appears low on the branches, or in fall, cut the plant back hard to about 6–12" to encourage vigorous, bushy growth.

Tips

The silvery foliage and blue flowers combine well with other plants in the back of a mixed border and soften the appearance of daylilies. Russian Sage may also be used to create a soft screen in a natural garden or on a dry bank.

Recommended

P. atriplicifolia is a loose, upright plant with silvery white, finely divided foliage. The small, lavender blue flowers are loosely held on silvery, branched stems. **'Filagran'** has delicate foliage and an upright habit. **'Longin'** is narrow and erect and has more smoothly edged leaves than other cultivars.

P. **'Blue Spire'** is an upright plant with deep blue flowers and feathery leaves.

'Filagran' (above), 'Longin' (below)

The airy habit of this plant creates a mist of silver purple in the garden.

Sea Holly
Eryngium

Height: 1–5' **Spread:** 12–24" **Flower color:** purple, blue, white
Blooms: summer to fall **Zones:** 4–8

IT'S TOUGH TO FIND PLANTS that thrive in hot, dry, sandy soil, but
that's where sea hollies really come alive in July and August. A number of
these plants are native to the United States. The most popular, Rattlesnake
Master, may be less showy than its relatives from Eastern Europe, but it is
said to cure rattlesnake bites and drive the slithery characters away. Does
it work? All I can tell you is that I grow this sea holly in my garden, and
I have never seen a rattlesnake lurking about.

Planting

Seeding: Not recommended, though direct sowing in fall may produce spring seedlings

Planting out: Spring

Spacing: 12–24"

Growing

Grow sea hollies in **full sun**. The soil should be **average to fertile** and **well drained**. These plants have a long taproot and are fairly drought tolerant, but they will suffer if left more than two weeks without water. Sea hollies are very slow to re-establish after dividing. Root cuttings can be taken in late winter.

The leaves of these plants are edged with small spines, making deadheading a pain—literally. It is not necessary unless you are very fussy about keeping plants neat.

E. x tripartitum (below)

Tips

Mix sea hollies with other late-season bloomers in a border. They make an interesting addition to naturalized gardens.

Recommended

E. alpinum (Alpine Sea Holly) grows 2–4' tall. This species has soft and feathery-looking but spiny bracts and steel blue or white flowers. There are several cultivars available in different shades of blue.

E. giganteum (Giant Sea Holly) grows 4–5' tall. The flowers are steel blue with silvery gray bracts.

E. x *tripartitum* grows 24–36" tall. The flowers are purple and the bracts are gray, tinged with purple.

E. varifolium (Moroccan Sea Holly) grows 12–16" tall. It has dark green leaves with silvery veins and gray-purple flowers with blue bracts.

E. x *tripartitum* (above),
E. alpinum (below)

E. yuccifolium (Rattlesnake Master) grows 3–4'
tall. This North American native forms a rosette
of long, narrow, spiny, blue-gray leaves. From
mid-summer to fall it bears creamy green or pale
blue flowers with gray-green bracts.

Problems & Pests

Roots may rot if the plants are left in standing
water for long periods of time. Slugs, snails and
powdery mildew may be problems.

The steel blue, globe-shaped flowerheads
come in a variety of sizes and are prized for
use in fresh and dried flower arrangements.
Long lasting but short stemmed, these
distinctive blooms must be mounted on
florists' wire.

E. giganteum (above)

Sedum
Stonecrop
Sedum

Height: 2–24" **Spread:** 18" to indefinite **Flower color:** yellow, white, red, pink; plant also grown for foliage **Blooms:** summer, fall **Zones:** 3–8

THIS LARGE AND DIVERSE GROUP includes deer-resistant, drought-tolerant plants ranging from 2" trailers to 12" uprights. Interesting bead-like, needle-thin or disk-shaped foliage in a wide array of colors—including red, pink, burgundy, purple, yellow, silver, golden and various greens—makes them fun to work with. Queen of the uprights, 'Autumn Joy' with its rose red, aging to brick red, flower clusters has become one of America's favorite plants. New varieties such as 'Brilliant' and 'Neon' are topped with brightly colored flowers in shades of pink.

Planting

Seeding: Sow indoors in early spring. Seed sold is often a mix of different species; you may not get what you expected, but you may be pleasantly surprised.

Planting out: Spring

Spacing: 18"

Growing

Sedums prefer **full sun** but tolerate partial shade. The soil should be of **average fertility**, very **well drained** and **neutral to alkaline**. Divide in spring when needed. Prune back 'Autumn Joy' in May by one-half and insert pruned-off parts into soft soil; cuttings root quickly. Early-summer pruning of upright species and hybrids yields compact, bushy plants but can delay flowering.

Tips

Low-growing sedums make great groundcovers and rock-garden or rock-wall plants. They also edge beds and borders beautifully. The taller types give a lovely late-season display in a bed or border.

Low-growing sedums make an excellent groundcover under trees. Their shallow roots survive well in the competition for space and moisture.

S. spurium 'Dragon's Blood'

Recommended

S. acre (Gold Moss Stonecrop) grows 2" high and spreads indefinitely. The small, yellow-green flowers are borne in summer.

S. 'Autumn Joy' (Autumn Joy Sedum) is a popular upright hybrid. The flowers open pink or red and later fade to deep bronze over a long period in late summer and fall. The plant forms a clump 24" tall, with an equal spread.

S. 'Mohrchen' forms an upright clump of stems. It grows about 24" tall, with an equal spread. Bronze red summer foliage brightens to ruby red in the fall. Clusters of pink flowers are borne in late summer and fall.

S. spectabile (Showy Stonecrop) is an upright species with pink flowers borne in late summer. It forms a clump 16–24" in height and spread.

S. 'Autumn Joy' (above),
S. spectabile 'Brilliant' (below)

'**Brilliant**' bears bright pink flowers. '**Neon**' has deep rosy pink flowers.

S. spurium (Two-row Stonecrop) forms a mat about 4" tall and 24" wide. The mid-summer flowers are deep pink or white. '**Dragon's Blood**' has bronze- or purple-tinged foliage and dark pink to dark red flowers. '**Fuldaglut**' bears red or rose pink flowers above orange-red or maroon foliage. '**Royal Pink**' has dark pink flowers and bright green foliage.

S. '**Vera Jameson**' is a low, mounding plant with purple-tinged stems and pinkish purple foliage. It grows up to 12" tall and spreads 18". Clusters of dark pink flowers are borne in late summer and fall.

S. 'Vera Jameson' (above),
S. 'Autumn Joy' (below)

Problems & Pests

Slugs, snails and scale insects may cause trouble for these plants.

'Autumn Joy' brings color to the late-season garden, when few flowers are in bloom.

Shasta Daisy
Leucanthemum

Height: 10–40" **Spread:** about 24" **Flower color:** white with yellow centers
Blooms: early summer to fall **Zones:** 4–9

THE BRIGHT WHITE, HAPPY FACE of Shasta Daisy has become a classic
in the American garden, having been hybridized by famous American
plantsman Luther Burbank in 1890. But too few gardeners try the double-
flowered varieties and some of the shorter selections. The unique, shaggy-
petaled look of 'Wirral Pride' stands out in the crowd, and the dwarf 'Snow
Lady' can brighten the front of the border.

Planting

Seeding: In spring, start seeds
indoors or direct sow; soil
temperature should be about
70–75° F

Planting out: Spring

Spacing: 24"

Growing

Shasta Daisy grows well in **full sun** and **partial shade**. The soil should be **fertile, moist** and **well drained**. Divide every year or two, in spring, to maintain plant vigor. Fall-planted Shasta Daisy may not become established in time to survive the winter. Plants can be short-lived in Zones 4 and 5.

Pinch or trim plants back in spring to encourage compact, bushy growth. Deadheading extends the bloom by several weeks.

Tips

Use this perennial in the border, where it can be grown as a single plant or massed in groups. The flowers can be cut for fresh arrangements.

Recommended

L. x *superbum* forms a large clump of dark green leaves and stems. It bears white, daisy-like flowers with yellow centers all summer, often until the first frost. 'Alaska' bears large flowers and is hardier than the species. 'Marconi' has large semi-double or double flowers. It should be protected from the hot afternoon sun. 'Silver Spoons' grows to about 40" tall and bears spidery flowers with long, narrow petals. 'Snow Lady' is a dwarf 10–14" tall with single flowers. 'Wirral Pride' bears double flowers composed of layers of fine, shaggy petals.

Problems & Pests

Occasional problems with aphids, leaf spot and leaf miners are possible.

Sneezeweed
Common Sneezeweed, Helen's Flower
Helenium

Height: 30"–6' **Spread:** 18–36" **Flower color:** red, orange, yellow, brown, maroon, bicolors **Blooms:** late summer, fall **Zones:** 3–9

WITH A NAME LIKE SNEEZEWEED, it's no wonder gardeners more often choose other plants to color up the fall garden. Too bad. The daisy-shaped flowers, with petals painted in blazing oranges, glorious golds and riveting reds, are unsurpassed when it comes to autumn color. Pinching these plants back every couple of weeks from May through mid-June produces more compact plants and increases flowering.

Planting
Seeding: Start seed indoors or out in spring. Cultivars do not come true to type.

Planting out: Spring or fall

Spacing: 18–36"

Helenium is named for Helen of Troy.

Growing

Sneezeweed grows best in **full sun**. The soil should be **fertile, moist** and **well drained**. Be sure to water well in summer. Divide every two or three years to keep clumps from becoming overgrown and dying out in the middle. Deadheading helps prolong the bloom.

Some support may be needed to hold mature stems upright. A peony hoop, shortened tomato cage or twiggy branches inserted into the soil in early spring while plants are still small will hold up the stems as they grow and will be hidden by the foliage as it matures. Pinch growth back in early summer to encourage lower, bushier growth that is less likely to need support.

Tips

Sneezeweed adds bright color to the border late in the season. It looks at home in informal cottage and meadow gardens. It will also work well near a pond or water feature, where it will get regular water.

No part of this plant should be eaten because it can upset your stomach. Sensitive individuals may get a rash or other skin irritation from contact with the leaves. Use gloves when handling.

Recommended

H. autumnale forms an upright clump of stems and narrow foliage. It bears yellow, red, brown, orange, maroon or bicolored, daisy-like flowers. '**Bruno**' bears mahogany flowers on compact plants 30"–4' tall, not quite the height of the species.

Problems & Pests

Powdery mildew can cause problems during dry spells.

Soapwort
Saponaria

Height: 3–24" **Spread:** 12–18" **Flower color:** pink, white, red
Blooms: spring, summer, fall **Zones:** 3–7

MOST SOAPWORTS SOLD in garden centers today are low plants that are covered in masses of dainty pink flowers. These athletic growers are best used where they will be kept in check. Their aggressiveness and ability to re-seed make them questionable for use in many gardens, but if you need to fill a large area of poor soil with an attractive, low-maintenance plant, a soapwort may be just what the doctor ordered. The upright version, naturalized throughout Michigan and often mistaken for Wild Phlox, is called Bouncing Bet because of its invasive tendencies.

Planting

Seeding: Start seeds indoors in early spring. Keep the planted seeds in a cool, dark place at about 60–65° F until they germinate. Move into a lighted room as soon as germination begins.

Planting out: Spring

Spacing: 18"

Saponin-rich plants such as S. officinalis *were used for cleaning purposes before commercially produced soap became available.*

Growing

Soapworts grow best in **full sun**. The soil should be of **average fertility, neutral to alkaline** and **well drained**. Poor soils are tolerated. Rich, fertile soil encourages lank, floppy growth. Divide in spring at least every two to three years to maintain vigor and control spread. Cut Rock Soapwort back after flowering to keep it neat and compact. Bouncing Bet requires regular deadheading to keep it looking tidy.

Tips

Use soapworts in borders, in rock gardens and on rock walls. Soapworts can overwhelm other plants.

Recommended

S. **'Bressingham'** grows up to 3" tall and spreads about 12". Its green foliage is topped with bright pink flowers in spring. This alpine type works well in the rock garden; it is not as invasive as other soapworts.

S. ocymoides (Rock Soapwort) forms a low, spreading mound. It grows 4–6" tall and spreads about 18".

The plant is completely covered in bright pink flowers in late spring and continues to flower sporadically all summer. 'Alba' has white flowers. 'Rubra Compacta' is very low growing, with dark pink flowers.

S. officinalis (Bouncing Bet, Soapwort) is an upright plant. It grows up to 24" tall and spreads about 18". This plant is aggressive, especially with good growing conditions. Pink, white or red flowers are borne from summer to fall. Cultivars are not as invasive as the species. **'Rosea Plena'** bears fragrant, pink double flowers in early summer.

S. officinalis 'Rosea Plena' (above),
S. ocymoides with 'Alba' (below)

Speedwell
Veronica
Veronica

Height: 6"–6' **Spread:** 12–24" **Flower color:** white, pink, purple, blue
Blooms: late spring, summer, fall **Zones:** 3–8

TREASURED FOR THEIR COLOR and staying power, the often blue flower spikes of speedwells persist for weeks. Though flopping is a problem for many varieties, shearing the plants back after flowering will tidy up the foliage and encourage re-blooming. In my herb garden, 'Blue Bouquet' produced scads of bright lavender blue spikes on strong branching stems with no sign of flopping.

Planting

Seeding: Not recommended; seedlings do not always come true to type. Seeds germinate quickly when started indoors in early spring.

Planting out: Spring

Spacing: 18"

Growing

Speedwells prefer **full sun** but tolerate partial shade. The soil should be of **average fertility, moist** and **well drained.** Lack of sun, and excessive moisture and nitrogen, may help explain the sloppy habits of some plants. Frequent dividing ensures strong, vigorous growth and decreases the likelihood of

flopping. Divide in fall or spring every two to three years.

When the spikes begin to fade, remove the entire spike to the point where it sprouted from the plant to encourage rapid re-blooming. For tidier plants, shear back to 6" in June.

Tips

Hungarian Speedwell is a beautiful plant for edging borders. Prostrate Speedwell is useful in a rock garden or at the front of a perennial border. Spike Speedwell works well in masses in a bed or border.

Recommended

V. austriaca **subsp.** *teucrium* (Hungarian Speedwell) forms a clump

V. spicata cultivar

that grows 6–24" tall and spreads 12–24". It bears spikes of bright blue flowers from late spring to mid-summer. 'Crater Lake Blue' grows 12–18" tall and bears deep blue flowers.

V. prostrata (Prostrate Speedwell) is a low-growing, spreading plant. It grows 6" tall and spreads 16". Its flowers may be blue or occasionally pink. Many cultivars are available.

V. spicata (Spike Speedwell) is a low, mounding plant with stems that flop over when they get too tall. It grows 12–24" tall, spreads 18" and bears spikes of blue flowers in summer.

Many cultivars of different colors are available. '**Blue Bouquet**' is a low-growing cultivar, to 12", with spikes of bright blue flowers. **Subsp.** *incana* has soft, hairy, silvery green leaves and deep purple-blue flowers. '**Red Fox**' has dark red-pink flowers.

Alternate Species

V. virginica (Culver's Root) has recently been re-named as a genus of its own, *Veronicastrum virginicum*, but it is still often grouped with the speedwells. This close relative is similar but much taller, with late summer and fall blooms. It grows 3–6' tall and spreads 12–24". Excessive

V. spicata 'Red Fox'

shade will cause the plants to flop over. Established plants tolerate short periods of drought. The flowers are borne on tall spikes and are most often white but may also be pale pink or pale purple. '**Album**' has attractive white flowers. '**Rosea**' has pale pink flowers. These are useful plants for the middle or back of the border and in situations where tall, narrow plants are needed.

Problems & Pests

Problems with scale insects are possible, as are fungal problems such as downy and powdery mildew, rust, leaf smut and root rot.

The genus name honors St. Veronica, who is said to have wiped the tears from the face of Jesus as he marched to Calvary.

V. virginica (below), V. spicata cultivar (right)

Spiderwort

Tradescantia

Height: 12–24" **Spread:** 18–24" **Flower color:** purple, blue, pink, red, white
Blooms: early summer to fall **Zones:** 3–9

SPIDERWORT IS A TOUGH-AS-NAILS PLANT with attractive grass-like foliage and brightly colored flowers. The leaves vary in color from bright green to blue-green to a bright and cheery chartreuse. The small, variously colored flowers last only a day, but they are self-cleaning and keep coming for eight weeks or more. For shaded areas choose shorter varieties to prevent flopping.

Planting
Seeding: Not recommended

Planting out: Spring or fall

Spacing: 18–24"

One of the parent plants of this hybrid, T. virginiana, *is native to most of the eastern United States.*

Growing

Spiderwort grows equally well in **full sun** or **partial shade**. The soil should be **fertile, humus rich** and **moist**. Divide in spring or fall every four or so years.

After flowering has ceased and the leaves fade, cutting the plants back will produce a fresh flush of foliage and possibly a second round of blooms late in the season. Dead-heading is not required during the flowering flush.

Tips

Spiderwort grows nicely in a well-watered border, and it looks very attractive next to a pond or other water feature, where the grassy foliage will soften the sometimes unnatural edges of the pond. This plant is also attractive in a lightly shaded woodland or natural garden.

Once established, Spiderwort will grow almost anywhere.

Recommended

T. x *andersoniana* (Andersoniana Hybrids) forms a large clump of grassy foliage. Clusters of three-petaled flowers are produced on long stems. '**Charlotte**' has pink flowers. '**Isis**' has bright blue flowers. '**Purple Dome**' has dark purple flowers. '**Red Cloud**' has red flowers. '**Snowcap**' has white flowers.

Problems & Pests

Problems are rarely severe enough to warrant control. Aphids, spider mites, caterpillars, rot and leaf spot may afflict plants from time to time.

A related species, Wandering Jew (T. zebrina), *is often grown as a trailing houseplant.*

Stokes' Aster
Stokesia

Height: 12–24" **Spread:** 12–18" **Flower color:** purple, blue, white, pink
Blooms: mid-summer to early fall **Zones:** 4–9

THESE BRIGHTLY COLORED, fringed, 3–4" wide blooms perched above glossy green foliage are stunners in the summer garden. The wide choice of colors, including blue, purple, pink and white, makes Stokes' Aster even more appealing for the front of borders. The soft blues of the flowers will complement and tone down the bright yellows of black-eyed Susans, Goldenrod and Sneezeweed.

Planting
Seeding: Start seeds indoors or out in fall with soil temperature at 70–75° F

Planting out: Spring

Spacing: 12"

The cornflower-like blooms can be cut for fresh arrangements.

Growing

Stokes' Aster grows best in **full sun**. The soil should be **average to fertile, light, moist** and **well drained**. This plant dislikes waterlogged and poorly drained soils, particularly in winter when root rot can quickly develop. Those who garden in clay might consider planting this species in raised beds filled with carefully amended soil. Provide a good winter mulch to protect the roots from the cycles of freezing and thawing, particularly in Zones 4 and 5. Divide in spring.

Deadheading extends the bloom, which can then last up to 12 weeks.

This lovely plant is native to the southeastern United States.

Tips

Stokes' Aster can be grouped in borders and adds some welcome blue tones to the garden late in the season, when yellows, oranges and golds seem to dominate.

Recommended

S. laevis forms a basal rosette of bright green, narrow foliage. The midvein of each leaf is a distinctive pale green. The plant bears purple, blue or sometimes white or pink flowers from mid-summer to early fall. **'Blue Danube'** bears large, purple-blue flowers. Cultivars with white or pink flowers can be difficult to locate.

Problems & Pests

Problems are rare, though leaf spot and caterpillars can cause problems. Avoid very wet and heavy soils to prevent root rot.

Sundrops
Evening Primrose
Oenothera

Height: 6–36" **Spread:** 12–18" **Flower color:** yellow, pink, white
Blooms: spring, summer, early fall **Zones:** 3–8

SUNDROPS ARE STAPLES in many perennial cottage gardens. Easy to grow, they bloom all summer and are lovely as cut flowers. The perfect plant, right? Not quite. These energetic bloomers multiply like crazy and will take over if you let them get the upper hand. But don't let that dissuade you from growing them, because they are perfect for narrow beds next to driveways and houses. Thinning them out in spring or fall keeps them under control.

Planting

Seeding: Start seeds in cold frame in mid-spring

Planting out: Spring

Spacing: 12"

Growing

Sundrops prefer **full sun**. The soil should be of **poor to average fertility** and very **well drained**. These plants can become invasive in a very fertile soil. They aren't bothered by hot, humid weather. Divide in spring.

Tips

Use these plants in the front of a border and to edge borders and pathways. Sundrops will brighten a gravelly bank or rock garden.

These plants can be a bit invasive, self-seeding readily and finding their way into unexpected places.

Recommended

O. fremontii bears yellow flowers over a long season. The foliage forms a mat 6" high and 12–18" wide. '**Lemon Silver**' is a recent introduction with silvery blue leaves and large, lemon yellow flowers.

O. fruticosa grows 18–36" tall and spreads 12–18". It bears bright yellow flowers in summer. The foliage will turn red after a light frost. '**Summer Solstice**' ('Sonnenwende') is a smaller, more compact plant. It bears larger flowers for a long period from early summer to early fall. The foliage turns red in summer and burgundy in fall.

O. speciosa (Showy Evening Primrose) is a lanky, upright or spreading plant. It grows 6–24" tall and spreads 12–18". Its flowers can be pink or white. '**Pinkie**' is a night-blooming plant with white flowers that mature to pink with darker pink veins.

Problems & Pests

Rare problems with downy mildew, powdery mildew, leaf gall, rust and leaf spot are possible. Root rot may develop in poorly drained soil.

Another common name for these plants is evening star, because at night the petals emit a phosphorescent light.

O. speciosa

Thrift
Sea Pink
Armeria

Height: 8–24" **Spread:** 12–24" **Flower color:** pink, white, purple, red
Blooms: late spring, summer **Zones:** 3–8

MANY MICHIGAN GARDENERS have overlooked these long-blooming, hardy little plants that thrive in lousy soil. The globe-shaped flowers in white and shades of pink dance over tufts of grass-like foliage for several weeks in summer, perking up rock gardens that are long on sun and short on water. The evergreen foliage adds color to the garden in winter.

Planting

Seeding: Start seeds indoors or out in spring or fall. Soak for a few hours before planting.

Planting out: Spring

Spacing: 10"

Growing

Thrift plants require **full sun**. The soil should be of **poor to moderate fertility, sandy** and **well drained**. These plants are very drought tolerant. Too fertile a soil or too much fertilizer reduces flowering and can kill the plants. Divide in spring or fall. Prompt deadheading extends the bloom.

Tips

These are useful plants for rock gardens or the front of a border.

If your thrift seems to be dying out in the middle of the clump, try cutting it back hard. New shoots should fill in quickly.

Recommended

A. maritima forms a clump of grassy foliage. Ball-like clusters of white, pink or purple flowers are borne at the ends of long stems in late spring and early summer. The plant grows up to 8" tall and spreads about 12". **'Alba'** has white flowers.

A. **'Bees'** is a group of larger hybrids that grow 18–24" tall, with an equal spread. The large white, pink or red flowers are borne in late spring and summer and are some of the most showy thrift blooms.

Problems & Pests

Problems are rare with the durable thrifts. They may occasionally come under attack by rust or aphids.

Attract bees and butterflies to your garden with clumps of thrift.

'Alba' (below)

Thyme
Thymus

Height: 2–18" **Spread:** 4–16" **Flower color:** purple, pink, white; plant grown mainly for foliage **Blooms:** late spring, summer **Zones:** 4–8

GARDENERS ARE DISCOVERING THE JOYS of these multi-faceted plants that were once relegated to the herb garden. Ground-hugging Woolly Thyme, with its lovely fuzzy, gray-green foliage, is a great choice for rock gardens. In summer the living carpet is covered with tiny pink flowers and the aromatic foliage tolerates light foot traffic. 'Albus' is covered with white flowers that glow in the summer garden at night, making a fabulous frame for stepping stones. Lemon-scented Thyme and all its variegated cultivars work beautifully as edging plants in beds and as foliage accents in containers.

Planting

Seeding: Many popular hybrids, particularly those with variegated leaves, cannot be grown from seed. Common Thyme and Mother of Thyme can be started from seed. Start indoors in early spring.

Planting out: Spring

Spacing: 16–20"

Growing

Thymes prefer **full sun.** The soil should be **average or poor** and very **well drained**; it helps to work leaf mold into it. Divide plants in spring.

It is easy to propagate thyme cultivars that cannot be started from seed. As the plant grows outwards, the branches touch the ground and send out new roots. These rooted stems may be removed and grown in pots to be planted out the following spring. Unrooted stem cuttings may be taken in early spring, before flowering.

T. serpyllum (this page)

This large genus has species throughout the world that were used in various ways in several cultures. Ancient Egyptians used thyme in embalming, the Greeks added it to baths and the Romans purified their rooms with it.

Tips

Thymes are useful plants for sunny, dry locations at the front of borders, between or beside paving stones and on rock gardens and rock walls.

Once the plants have finished flowering, it is a good idea to shear them back by about half to encourage new growth and prevent the plants from becoming too woody.

Recommended

T. x *citriodorus* (Lemon-scented Thyme) forms a mound 12" tall and 10" wide. The foliage has a lemon scent, and the flowers are pale pink. The cultivars are more ornamental. **'Argenteus'** has silver-edged leaves. **'Aureus'** has leaves with golden yellow variegation. **'Golden King'** has yellow-margined leaves.

T. pseudolanguinosus (Woolly Thyme) is a mat-forming plant up

T. x *citriodorus* 'Argenteus' (above),
T. vulgaris (below)

to 3" high and 8–10" in spread, with fuzzy, gray-green leaves. It bears pink or purplish flowers in summer.

T. serpyllum (Mother of Thyme, Creeping Thyme, Wild Thyme) is a popular low-growing species. It usually grows about 5" tall and spreads 12" or more. The flowers are purple. There are many cultivars available. **'Albus'** (White Creeping Thyme) bears white flowers. **'Elfin'** forms tiny, dense mounds up to 2–3" tall and 4" in spread. It rarely flowers. **'Minimus'** grows 2" high and 4" wide. **'Snowdrift'** has white flowers.

T. vulgaris (Common Thyme) forms a bushy mound of dark green leaves. It usually grows about 12–18" tall and spreads about 16". The flowers may be purple, pink or white. **'Silver Posie'** is a good cultivar that has pale pink flowers and silver-edged leaves.

Problems & Pests

Thyme plants rarely have problems. Seedlings may suffer from damping off and plants may get gray mold or root rot. Good circulation and adequate drainage are good ways to avoid these problems.

In the Middle Ages, it was believed that drinking a thyme infusion would enable one to see fairies.

T. serpyllum (above),
T. x citriodorus 'Golden King' (below)

Trillium
Wake Robin
Trillium

Height: 16–20" **Spread:** 12" or more **Flower color:** white, yellow, pink, red, purple **Blooms:** spring **Zones:** 4–7

THE FIRST PLANTS most gardeners think of when planning a woodland garden are trilliums. These beautiful Michigan natives are easy to grow once their simple needs are met. Plant in a shaded area in fertile, humus-rich soil that remains moderately moist all season. Should the soil dry out for a time, trilliums will go dormant but not necessarily die, so don't dig them out if they suddenly disappear. Happy companions include primroses, bleeding hearts, Empimedium, Bloodroot and Virginia Bluebells.

Planting

Seeding: Not recommended; may take two or more years before signs of growth and another five or more years before plants reach flowering size. Ripe seeds may be started in a shaded cold frame in late summer.

Planting out: Fall or spring

Spacing: 12"

Growing

Locate trilliums in **full or partial shade**. The soil should be **humus rich, moist, well drained** and **neutral** or **acidic**. Rhizomes should be planted about 4" deep. Add organic matter, such as compost or aged manure, to the soil when planting and add a mulch of shredded leaves to encourage rapid growth. Division is not necessary.

Tips

These plants are ideal for woodland gardens or plantings under spring-flowering trees and shrubs.

Trilliums are best left alone once planted. Newly transplanted plants may take a year or two to adjust and start flowering. The amount of moisture they receive after flowering greatly influences how quickly the plants become established. Plentiful moisture in summer prevents the plants from going dormant after flowering. Instead, they send up side shoots that increase the size of the clump and the number of flowers the following spring.

Recommended

T. erectum (Purple Trillium) has deep wine red flowers. It grows up to 20" tall and spreads up to 12".

T. grandiflorum (Great White Trillium) has large white flowers that turn pink as they fade. It grows 16" tall and spreads 12" or more. '**Flore Pleno**' has double flowers but is slower growing.

T. recurvatum (Purple Wake Robin, Purple Trillium) has dark purple or occasionally yellow or white flowers. It grows up to 16" tall and spreads 12".

Problems & Pests

Trilliums have few pest problems, but the young foliage may be attacked by slugs and snails.

Be sure to purchase trilliums from a reputable nursery. Wild populations of these hard-to-propagate plants have been severely depleted by collectors.

T. grandiflorum

Vinca
Myrtle, Periwinkle
Vinca

Height: 4–8" **Spread:** indefinite **Flower color:** blue, purple, white
Blooms: mid-spring, fall **Zones:** 4–9

WHEN IT COMES TO GROUNDCOVERS, Vinca vies
with Pachysandra for the top spot in Michigan gardens.
Vinca grows well in most soils and heralds the arrival
of spring with a bounty of blue flowers. It will
re-bloom sporadically in fall. A number of new
varieties are now available with variegated
foliage that helps brighten shaded areas.
'Ralph Shugert,' the handsome sport of
'Bowles Variety,' was registered right
here in Michigan by horticulturist
David Mackenzie, owner of
Hortec of Indian Lake.

*The glossy green foliage
of Vinca remains
attractive and cooling in
the heat of summer, long
after the early flush of
flowers has finished.*

Planting
Seeding: Not recommended
Planting out: Spring or fall
Spacing: 24–36"

Growing

Grow Vinca in **partial to full shade**. It will grow in **any type of soil** as long as it is not too dry. The plants turn yellow if the soil is too dry or the sun too hot. Divide Vinca in early spring or mid- to late fall, whenever it becomes overgrown. One plant can cover almost any area.

After planting, mulch the soil surface with shredded leaves and compost to prevent weeds from sprouting among the groundcover. The mulch will also help keep the soil moist to hasten Vinca's establishment and encourage it to fill in quickly.

Tips

Vinca makes a useful and attractive groundcover in a shrub border, under trees or on a shady bank, and it prevents soil erosion. Vinca is shallow-rooted and able to out-compete weeds but won't interfere with deeper-rooted shrubs.

If Vinca begins to outgrow its space, shear it back hard in early spring. If the sheared-off ends have rooted along the stems, these cuttings may be potted and given away as gifts or planted in new areas of the garden.

Recommended

V. minor (Lesser Periwinkle) forms a low, loose mat of trailing stems. Purple or blue flowers are borne in a flush in spring and sporadically all summer and into fall. 'Alba' bears white flowers. '**Atropurpurea**' bears reddish purple flowers. '**Blue and Gold**' has vibrant bluish purple flowers and medium green leaves with wide edges of bright golden yellow. '**Bowles Variety**' ('LaGrave') bears large purple-blue flowers. '**Ralph Shugert**' has dark, glossy, silver-edged leaves and purple-blue flowers, larger than those of the species.

The Romans used the long, trailing stems of Vinca to make wreaths. This use of the plant may explain its name, which is derived from the Latin vincire, *'to bind.'*

'Ralph Shugert'

Wild Ginger
Asarum

Height: 3–6" **Spread:** 12" or more **Flower color:** burgundy or green, not showy; plant grown for foliage **Blooms:** early summer **Zones:** 4–8

WILD GINGERS ARE WOODLAND SPECIES that thrive in moist but well-drained, acidic soil. Their cyclamen-like foliage is prized by those who love to add both texture and a variegated look to woodland plantings. Most are slow growers that take two to three years to develop into spectacular clumps, so be patient with them. Tender varieties may be grown as container plants that spend the winter indoors.

Planting

Seeding: Not recommended

Planting out: Spring or fall

Spacing: 12"

Growing

Wild gingers need **full shade** or **partial shade**. The soil should be **moist** and **humus rich**. All *Asarum* species prefer **acidic** soils, but *A. canadense* will tolerate alkaline conditions. Wild gingers tolerate dry conditions for a while in good shade, but prolonged drought will eventually cause the plants to wilt and die back. Division is unlikely to be necessary, except to propagate more plants.

Tips

Use wild gingers in a shady rock garden, border or woodland garden.

The thick, fleshy rhizomes grow along the soil or just under it, and pairs of leaves grow up from the rhizomes. Cuttings can be made by removing sections of rhizome with leaves growing from them and planting each section separately. When taking cuttings, you must be careful not to damage the tiny thread-like roots that grow from the stem below the point where the leaves attach.

Recommended

A. canadense (Canada Wild Ginger) is native to eastern North America. The heart-shaped leaves are slightly hairy.

A. europaeum (European Wild Ginger) is a European native with very glossy leaves, often distinctively silver-veined. It is the quickest species to spread over an area but is not as heat tolerant as *A. canadense*.

The heart-shaped leaves can be tucked into simple flower arrangements.

A. canadense (this page)

Canada Wild Ginger rhizomes have a distinctive ginger scent. This plant is not related to the common culinary ginger (Zingiber officinale), *but the rhizomes may be used as a similar flavoring in many dishes.*

Yarrow
Achillea

Height: 4"–4' **Spread:** 12–36" **Flower color:** white, yellow, red, orange, pink, purple **Blooms:** summer, fall **Zones:** 3–9

SOME GARDENERS DISMISS YARROWS as invasive pests, but many varieties are well behaved and can become valued additions to the perennial garden. Planted in masses, these hardy, reliable, easy-care plants with their colorful, long-lasting flowers—hordes of tiny blossoms clustered into flat heads—are showstoppers. As their colors soften and fade with age, the blooms of yellow, red and deep pink yarrow cultivars will become a rich tapestry. If deer are devastating your garden, add color to your borders with yarrows and other deer-resistant plants such as speedwells and Bergamot.

Planting
Seeding: Direct sow in spring. Don't cover the seeds; they need light to germinate.

Planting out: Spring

Spacing: 12–24"

Growing

Grow in **full sun**. Yarrows do well in an **average to sandy** soil that is **well drained**. These plants tolerate drought and poor soil but do not do well in a heavy, wet soil or in very humid conditions. Excessively rich soil or too much nitrogen results in weak, floppy growth. Good drainage is key to survival of these plants. *A. millefolium* and *A. filipendulina* often need staking. Divide every two or three years, in spring.

Once the flowerheads begin to fade, cut them back to the lateral buds. Yarrows will flower more profusely and longer if they are deadheaded. Basal foliage should be left in place over the winter and tidied up in spring.

A. ptarmica 'The Pearl' (above), *A. millefolium* cultivar with *Phlox* (below)

The ancient Druids used yarrow to divine seasonal weather, and the ancient Chinese used the stems to foretell the future.

Tips

Yarrows are informal plants. Cottage gardens, wildflower gardens and mixed borders are perfect places to grow them. These plants thrive in hot, dry locations where nothing else will grow.

Yarrow plants make excellent groundcovers, despite being quite tall. The plants send up shoots from a low basal point and may be mowed periodically without excessive damage to the plant. Mower blades should be kept at least 4" high. Do not mow more often than once a month, or you will have short yarrow with no flowers!

Yarrows are used in fresh and dried arrangements. Pick flowerheads only after pollen is visible or they will die very quickly once cut.

Recommended

A. 'Anthea' bears bright yellow flowers that fade to creamy yellow. It will flower all summer if kept deadheaded. The foliage is silvery gray. Plants grow 12–24" tall and spread 12–18".

A. filipendulina has yellow flowers and grows up to 4' tall. It has been used to develop several hybrids and cultivars. Cultivars come in various heights, with flowers in shades of yellow. 'Coronation Gold' has bright golden yellow flowers and fern-like foliage. It grows about 36" tall, with a 12" spread. This cultivar is quite heat tolerant.

A. x *lewisii* 'King Edward' is a low-growing hybrid with woolly gray leaves. It grows 4–8" tall and spreads about 12". It bears clusters of yellow flowers in early summer.

A. millefolium (Common Yarrow) grows 12–36" tall, with an equal spread, and has white flowers. The foliage is soft and very finely divided. Because it is quite aggressive, the species is almost never grown in favor of the many cultivars that have been developed. 'Cerise Queen' has pinkish red flowers. 'Fireland' bears red flowers with yellow centers; the flowers mature to coppery salmon and then soft gold. 'Summer Pastels' has flowers of many colors, including white, yellow, pink and purple. This is a very heat- and drought-tolerant cultivar and has fade-resistant flowers. 'Terra Cotta' bears flowers that open orangy pink and mature to rusty orange.

A. 'Moonshine' bears bright yellow flowers all summer. The foliage is silvery gray. The plant grows 18–24" tall and spreads 12–24".

A. millefolium cultivar

A. ptarmica (Sneezewort) grows
12–24" tall, with an equal spread.
It bears clusters of white flowers all
summer. 'The Pearl' bears clusters
of white, button-like double flowers.
This cultivar can become invasive.
It can be started from seed, but not
all seedlings will come true to type.

Problems & Pests

Rare problems with powdery
mildew and stem rot are possible.

*Yarrows have blood-coagulating
properties that were recognized
by the ancient Greeks.* Achillea
*is named after the legendary
Achilles, because during the
battle of Troy he is said to have
treated his warriors' wounds
with this herb.*

A. filipendulina (above),
cultivar with *Artemisia* & *Echinacea* (below)

Other Perennials to Consider

Balloon Flower
Platycodon grandiflorus
Forms an upright clump or a low mound. Features balloon-like buds opening to large blue, white or pink flowers. Grows 18–36" tall; some dwarf cultivars, e.g., 'Sentimental Blue,' grow only 6–8" tall. Spread 12–18" in both cases. Blooms mid- to late summer. Grows well in **full sun** or **partial shade** with **average to fertile, light, moist, well-drained** soil. Amend heavy clay with sphagnum peat, compost and gravel to improve drainage. Plant resents being divided or having roots disturbed. Pinch in early summer to encourage bushier, less floppy growth, and deadhead to prolong blooming. Mark plant in the fall because it sprouts late in spring. Use in borders, rock gardens and cottage gardens. (Zones 3–8)

Bear's Breeches
Acanthus spinosus
Large, clump-forming perennial 3–5' tall with equal spread. Bears spiny leaves and attractive, bicolored purple and white flowers on tall spikes. Blooms late spring to mid-summer. Grow in **partial or light shade** in any **well-drained** soil. Drought tolerant once established. Can become invasive in too loose a soil. Divide frequently, in fall or early spring, to keep plants vigorous; wear gloves when dividing. Mulch heavily in winter. Dramatic plant for middle or back of borders. Blooms make a lovely addition to fresh arrangements, but watch out for the spines. (Zones 5–10)

Checkermallow
Sidalcea malviflora
Upright plant 2–4' tall and 12–18" wide. Resembles Hollyhock, with a basal rosette of foliage and tall spikes of flowers in shades of pink, but this plant is more disease resistant, needs less staking and can live longer. 'Party Girl' is a dwarf 24" tall. Checkermallow blooms most of summer if deadheaded regularly. Prefers **full sun** but tolerates partial shade. Soil should be **fertile, sandy, humus rich, acidic, moist** and **well drained,** but plant adapts to all but waterlogged soils. Water regularly, and mulch heavily for winter. Divide in spring or fall. Useful in groups at back or middle of borders. (Zones 5–7; possibly Zone 4 with protection)

Sidalcea malviflora

Corydalis lutea

Corydalis
Corydalis lutea
Low, mound-forming perennial
12–18" tall and 12" or more in
spread, with attractive, ferny foliage
and small yellow flowers. '**Blue
Panda**' bears bright, sky blue flowers. Corydalis blooms late spring to
mid-summer. Grows well in **partial
or light shade** with **average, humus-
rich, well-drained** soil. If plant fades
by mid-summer, shear back to
encourage fresh growth. Corydalis
can self-seed aggressively but
seedlings not difficult to pull up
if necessary. Division not recommended. Useful in woodland and
shaded rock gardens, as edging
along paths and for naturalizing
in underused areas. Grows well
between rocks in paths and walls.
(Zones 4–7)

False Solomon's Seal
Smilacina racemosa
Native woodland perennial; forms a
spreading clump of upright, arching
stems. Grows up to 36" tall and 2–4'

wide; bears plume-like clusters of
white flowers at ends of stems in
mid- to late spring. Berries ripen to
bright red in late summer and fall.
Prefers **light or full shade** and **average, humus-rich, moist, well-
drained** soil with peat moss added.
Divide in spring if necessary to
propagate. Useful in open woodland
or natural gardens and in shaded
borders with hostas and other shade
lovers. (Zones 3–7)

Feverfew
Tanacetum parthenium
Bushy plant with fern-like foliage;
grows 18–36" tall and spreads
12–18". Clusters of small, daisy-like,
yellow or white flowers with yellow
centers are produced mid-summer
to fall. '**Aureum**' has bright yellow-
green foliage. Feverfew grows well in
full sun with any **average, well-
drained** soil. Deadheading prolongs
blooming, but leave some flowers in
place to self-seed because plant can
be short-lived. Divide in spring as
often as needed to keep plant vigorous. Useful in borders, rock gardens,
cottage gardens and meadow gardens. (Zones 5–8; to Zone 3 with
winter protection)

Tanacetum parthenium

Solidago 'Crown of Rays'

Goldenrod

Solidago hybrids

Hybrids bred for more attractive flowers than the common wild goldenrods. Plants form a clump of strong stems 24–36" tall and about 18" wide, with narrow leaves. Plumes of bright yellow flowers appear midsummer to fall. **'Crown of Rays'** has horizontally oriented flower sprays; **'Golden Shower'** has more pendent flower sprays. Goldenrods prefer **full sun** but tolerate some shade. **Poor to average, light, well-drained** soil is best. Too-fertile soil encourages green growth but not flowers. Divide in spring or fall to control growth and keep plants vigorous. Useful for late-season color in large borders, cottage gardens and wildflower gardens. May overwhelm other plants. (Zones 3–7)

Many people falsely associate goldenrod flowers with hayfever. The inconspicuous flowers of Ragweed, which blooms at the same time, are actually responsible.

Jacob's Ladder

Polemonium caeruleum

Forms dense clump of basal foliage from which leafy upright stems emerge, topped with clusters of purple, blue or white flowers. Grows 18–36" tall with an equal spread. **'Brise d'Anjou'** has leaves with creamy white margins. Jacob's Ladder blooms late spring and early summer. Grows well in **full sun** or **partial shade** with **fertile, humus-rich, moist, well-drained** soil. Division rarely required but can be done in late summer for propagation. Self-seeds readily. Useful in borders and woodland gardens. (Zones 3–7)

Jupiter's Beard

Centranthus ruber

Bushy, upright plant 24–36" tall and 12–24" wide. Bears large clusters of red, pink or white flowers that bloom on and off all summer with regular deadheading. Grows best in **full sun** with **average, neutral to alkaline, well-drained** soil. Division not required but can be done in spring or fall to propagate plants. Useful in borders. Can be left to self-seed a sea of bright red flowers in an unused corner. Blooms are attractive in fresh arrangements. (Zones 4–8)

Centranthus ruber

Masterwort

Astrantia major

Newcomer to Michigan gardens. Forms a clump of deeply lobed foliage 12–36" tall and about 18" in spread. Bears clusters of pink, green, red or purple flowers surrounded by stiff green, white or pink bracts. 'Rubra' bears deep maroon flowers. Masterwort blooms all summer. Prefers **light or partial shade** and **fertile, humus-rich, moist** soil. Tolerates full sun in consistently moist soil; tolerates periodically dry soil in shade. Self-seeds abundantly in a good location, so deadhead if you don't want dozens of plants. Divide in spring or fall. Useful in woodland gardens or next to water features. Should be kept well watered if grown in borders. Flowers long-lasting in fresh arrangements. (Zones 4–7)

Pachysandra

Pachysandra terminalis

Forms a low, spreading mass of evergreen foliage rosettes about 6–12" tall with indefinite spread. Bears small spikes of fairly inconspicuous flowers in spring. Prefers **light to full shade** with **moist,**

Astrantia major 'Rubra'

humus-rich, well-drained soil. Generally needs little attention; shear back winter-damaged growth in spring to encourage flush of new growth. Division not required but can be done in spring for propagation. Useful as durable groundcover for under trees, along north-facing walls, in shady borders and in woodland gardens. (Zones 4–9)

Potentilla

Potentilla nepalensis

Most gardeners know the common shrubby potentillas but may not be as familiar with the attractive perennial species. *P. nepalensis* grows 12–18" tall, with trailing stems that spread up to 24". Bears rose pink flowers from late spring to early summer. **'Miss Willmott'** bears scarlet flowers with contrasting dark red centers. Potentilla grows well in **full sun** or **partial shade** with **poor to average, well-drained** soil. Drought tolerant when protected from hot afternoon sun. Divide in spring or fall, when center of plant appears to be thinning or dying out. Useful in borders, in rock gardens and on rock walls. Shear back 'Miss Willmott' after flowering to keep it neat and tidy and perhaps encourage a late-season flush of flowers. (Zones 3–8)

Pachysandra terminalis

Sweet Woodruff

Galium odoratum

Low, spreading groundcover 6–12" tall with an indefinite spread. Bears clusters of white, star-shaped flowers in a flush in late spring; continues to bloom sporadically till mid-summer. Grows well in **partial or light shade** with **humus-rich**, evenly **moist** soil. Does not flower as well in full shade. Shear back lightly after flowering to encourage plants to fill in with foliage and crowd out weeds. Divide in spring or fall. Useful in woodland gardens or shrub borders as groundcover. Dried leaves once used to scent doorways and freshen stale rooms. (Zones 3–8)

White Gaura

Gaura lindheimeri

Forms a large, bushy clump 3–5' tall and 24–36" in spread. Bears loose spikes of white or pinkish flowers on long, slender stems. Only a few of

Galium odoratum

the flowers open at once, but plants bloom from late spring to early fall. 'Whirling Butterflies' is more compact, 24–36" tall, with white flowers. Prefers **full sun** with **fertile, moist, well-drained** soil. Drought tolerant once established. Should not sit in wet soil in winter. Improve drainage by adding sharp sand and compost to soil. Deadhead to prolong blooming. Division not needed; plants dislike having roots disturbed. Likely to self-seed. New plants can be moved carefully when small. Use as filler in mixed borders or naturalize on a dry slope. (Zones 5–8)

Willow-Leaved Sunflower

Helianthus salicifolius

Perennial sunflower related to the annual species. Forms large, upright clump of stems up to 8' tall and about 36" wide, with narrow leaves. Bears many yellow, daisy-like, brown-centered flowers in late summer and fall. Grows well in **full sun** with **average, neutral to alkaline, moist, well-drained** soil. Likes regular watering but quite drought tolerant once established. Cut back hard after bloom. Divide every three or so years in spring or fall to keep plant vigorous. Useful at back or center of borders. Can be used in dry and underwatered areas and to provide a quick-growing privacy screen. (Zones 4–8)

Willow-leaved Sunflower is in the same genus as the annual sunflowers (H. annuus), *but the perennial version has smaller, more plentiful flowers.*

Gardens to Visit in Michigan

ANN ARBOR: UNIVERSITY OF MICHIGAN

Matthaei Botanical Gardens and Conservatory
(734) 998-7061

BLOOMFIELD HILLS

Cranbrook House and Gardens
(248) 645-3149

EAST LANSING: MICHIGAN STATE UNIVERSITY

4-H Children's Garden
(517) 355-0348

Clarence E. Lewis Landscape Arboretum (517) 355-0348

Horticultural Demonstration Gardens (517) 355-0348

W.J. Beal Botanical Garden
(517) 355-9582

DEARBORN

Greenfield Village
(800) 835-5237

DETROIT

Anna Scripps Whitcomb Conservatory, Belle Isle
(313) 852-4065

Detroit Garden Center
(313) 259-6363

DRYDEN

Seven Ponds Nature Center
(810) 796-3200

GRAND RAPIDS

Frederik Meijer Gardens
(888) 957-1580

GROSSE POINTE SHORES

Edsel and Eleanor Ford House
(313) 884-4222

MIDLAND

Dow Gardens
(800) 362-4874

NILES

Fernwood Botanic Garden and Nature Center
(616) 695-6491

TIPTON

Hidden Lake Gardens
(517) 431-2060

Jacob's Ladder

Height Legend: Low: < 12" • Medium: 12–24" • Tall: > 24"

SPECIES by Common Name	White	Pink	Red	Orange	Yellow	Blue	Purple	Foliage	Spring	Summer	Fall	Low	Medium	Tall
	COLOR								BLOOMING			HEIGHT		
Ajuga	*	*				*	*	*	*	*		*		
Anemone	*	*			*	*			*	*	*	*	*	*
Artemisia	*				*			*		*		*	*	*
Aster	*	*	*			*	*			*	*	*	*	*
Astilbe	*	*	*	*			*	*		*		*	*	*
Basket-of-gold				*	*				*			*	*	
Bellflower	*	*				*	*		*	*		*	*	*
Bergamot		*	*				*		*					*
Bergenia	*	*	*				*	*	*				*	
Black-eyed Susan			*	*	*					*	*		*	*
Blanket Flower			*	*	*					*	*		*	*
Blazing Star	*						*			*			*	*
Bleeding Heart	*	*	*				*		*	*			*	*
Boltonia	*	*					*			*	*			*
Brunnera						*			*				*	
Butterfly Weed	*		*	*	*					*	*		*	*
Candytuft	*								*			*		
Cardinal Flower	*	*	*		*	*				*	*			*
Catmint	*	*				*	*		*	*	*	*	*	*
Chrysanthemum	*	*	*	*	*		*			*	*		*	*
Clematis	*	*	*		*	*	*			*			*	*
Columbine	*	*	*		*	*	*		*	*			*	*
Coral Bells	*	*	*		*		*		*	*			*	*
Coreopsis		*		*	*					*			*	*
Cornflower	*	*				*	*		*	*			*	
Crocosmia			*	*	*					*			*	*
Daylily		*	*	*	*		*		*	*			*	*
Dead Nettle	*	*			*		*	*	*	*		*	*	
Delphinium	*	*				*	*		*	*				*

	LIGHT				SOIL CONDITIONS								SPECIES by Common Name
Sun	Part Shade	Light Shade	Shade	Moist	Well Drained	Dry	Fertile	Average	Poor	USDA Zones	Page Number	
*	*	*	*		*		*	*	*	3–8	68	Ajuga
*	*	*		*	*		*	*		5–8	72	Anemone
*					*		*	*		3–8	76	Artemisia
*	*			*	*		*			3–8	80	Aster
	*	*	*	*	*		*			3–9	84	Astilbe
*				*	*	*		*	*	3–7	88	Basket-of-gold
*	*	*		*	*		*	*		3–7	92	Bellflower
*	*	*		*	*		*			3–9	96	Bergamot
*	*				*		*	*		3–8	100	Bergenia
*	*				*			*		3–9	104	Black-eyed Susan
*					*		*			3–10	106	Blanket Flower
*				*	*			*		3–9	108	Blazing Star
	*	*	*	*	*		*			3–9	110	Bleeding Heart
*	*			*	*	*	*	*		4–9	114	Boltonia
	*	*		*	*			*		3–8	116	Brunnera
*					*	*	*	*	*	4–9	118	Butterfly Weed
*				*	*			*	*	3–9	120	Candytuft
*	*	*		*			*			3–9	122	Cardinal Flower
*	*				*			*		3–8	126	Catmint
*				*	*		*			5–9	130	Chrysanthemum
*	*			*	*		*			3–8	134	Clematis
*	*			*	*		*			2–9	138	Columbine
	*	*		*	*		*	*		3–9	142	Coral Bells
*				*	*			*		3–9	146	Coreopsis
*		*		*	*			*	*	3–8	150	Cornflower
*				*	*			*		5–9	152	Crocosmia
*	*	*	*	*	*	*	*	*		2–9	154	Daylily
*	*	*		*	*			*		3–8	158	Dead Nettle
*				*	*		*			3–7	162	Delphinium

Height Legend: Low: < 12" • Medium: 12–24" • Tall: > 24"

SPECIES by Common Name	White	Pink	Red	Orange	Yellow	Blue	Purple	Foliage	Spring	Summer	Fall	Low	Medium	Tall
	COLOR								BLOOMING			HEIGHT		
Euphorbia				*	*			*	*	*			*	
False Indigo						*	*			*				*
False Sunflower				*	*					*	*			*
Foamflower	*	*							*	*		*		
Foxglove	*	*	*		*		*		*	*				*
Geum			*	*	*					*			*	
Globe Thistle						*	*	*		*				*
Goat's Beard	*							*		*		*	*	*
Golden Marguerite	*				*				*	*		*	*	*
Hardy Geranium	*	*	*			*	*	*		*		*	*	*
Hens and Chicks	*		*		*		*	*		*		*		
Hollyhock	*	*	*	*	*		*			*	*			*
Hosta	*						*	*		*	*	*	*	*
Iris	*	*	*		*	*	*		*	*		*	*	*
Joe-Pye Weed	*	*					*	*		*	*			*
Lady's Mantle					*			*		*	*	*	*	
Lamb's Ears		*					*	*		*		*	*	
Lavender		*					*			*		*	*	*
Ligularia				*	*			*		*	*			*
Lungwort	*	*	*				*	*	*			*	*	
Lychnis	*	*	*	*						*				*
Mallow	*	*				*	*			*	*	*	*	*
Meadow Rue	*	*			*		*		*	*				*
Meadowsweet	*	*						*	*	*				*
Monkshood	*					*	*			*				*
Obedient Plant	*	*					*			*	*		*	*
Oriental Poppy	*	*	*	*					*	*			*	*
Penstemon	*	*	*		*		*		*	*	*		*	*
Peony	*	*	*		*		*	*		*				*

LIGHT				SOIL CONDITIONS						USDA Zones	Page Number	SPECIES by Common Name
Sun	Part Shade	Light Shade	Shade	Moist	Well Drained	Dry	Fertile	Average	Poor			
*		*		*	*	*		*		4–9	166	Euphorbia
*	*				*	*		*	*	3–9	170	False Indigo
*	*			*	*		*	*		2–9	172	False Sunflower
	*	*		*			*			3–8	174	Foamflower
	*	*		*			*			3–8	176	Foxglove
*				*	*		*			3–7	180	Geum
*	*				*	*		*	*	3–8	182	Globe Thistle
	*	*	*	*			*			3–7	184	Goat's Beard
*					*	*		*		3–7	188	Golden Marguerite
*	*	*	*	*	*	*		*		3–8	190	Hardy Geranium
*	*				*			*	*	3–8	194	Hens and Chicks
*	*	*			*			*		3–7	196	Hollyhock
*	*	*	*	*	*		*	*		3–8	200	Hosta
*		*		*	*			*		3–10	204	Iris
*	*			*			*			3–9	208	Joe-Pye Weed
	*	*		*	*	*	*			3–7	210	Lady's Mantle
*					*	*		*	*	3–8	214	Lamb's Ears
*					*		*	*		5–9	216	Lavender
	*	*		*				*		4–8	220	Ligularia
	*	*	*	*	*		*			3–8	224	Lungwort
*	*				*			*		3–8	228	Lychnis
*	*			*	*	*		*		4–9	230	Mallow
	*	*		*	*		*	*		3–8	234	Meadow Rue
	*	*		*			*			3–8	238	Meadowsweet
	*	*		*			*	*		3–8	242	Monkshood
*	*	*		*			*	*		2–9	246	Obedient Plant
*					*		*	*		3–7	248	Oriental Poppy
*	*				*	*	*	*		4–8	250	Penstemon
*	*			*	*		*			2–7	254	Peony

Height Legend: Low: < 12" • Medium: 12–24" • Tall: > 24"

SPECIES by Common Name	White	Pink	Red	Orange	Yellow	Blue	Purple	Foliage	Spring	Summer	Fall	Low	Medium	Tall
	COLOR								BLOOMING			HEIGHT		
Phlox	*	*	*	*		*	*		*	*	*	*	*	*
Pincushion Flower	*	*				*	*			*			*	
Pinks	*	*	*				*		*	*		*	*	
Plume Poppy	*							*		*				*
Primrose	*	*	*	*	*	*	*		*	*		*	*	
Purple Coneflower	*	*		*			*			*			*	*
Red-hot Poker	*		*	*	*					*				*
Rockcress	*	*							*			*		
Rodgersia	*	*	*							*				*
Rose Mallow	*	*	*							*	*		*	*
Russian Sage						*	*			*	*			*
Sea Holly	*					*	*	*		*	*		*	*
Sedum	*	*	*		*			*		*	*	*	*	
Shasta Daisy	*				*					*	*		*	*
Sneezeweed			*	*	*					*	*			*
Soapwort	*	*	*						*	*	*	*	*	
Speedwell	*	*				*	*		*	*		*	*	
Spiderwort	*	*	*			*	*			*	*		*	
Stokes' Aster	*	*				*	*			*	*		*	
Sundrops	*	*			*				*	*		*	*	*
Thrift	*	*							*	*		*	*	
Thyme	*	*					*	*	*	*		*	*	
Trillium	*	*	*		*				*				*	
Vinca	*		*			*	*	*	*	*	*	*		
Wild Ginger			*				*	*		*		*		
Yarrow	*	*	*	*	*			*		*	*		*	*

LIGHT				SOIL CONDITIONS						USDA Zones	Page Number	SPECIES by Common Name
Sun	Part Shade	Light Shade	Shade	Moist	Well Drained	Dry	Fertile	Average	Poor			
*	*			*	*		*			3–8	258	Phlox
*	*				*		*	*		3–7	262	Pincushion Flower
*		*			*	*		*		3–9	264	Pinks
*	*			*	*	*		*	*	3–10	268	Plume Poppy
	*	*		*	*		*	*		3–8	270	Primrose
*		*		*	*	*	*	*		3–8	274	Purple Coneflower
*				*	*		*			5–9	276	Red-hot Poker
*					*			*	*	4–7	278	Rockcress
	*	*		*			*			5–7	280	Rodgersia
*				*			*	*		4–9	282	Rose Mallow
*					*			*	*	4–9	284	Russian Sage
*					*	*	*	*		4–8	286	Sea Holly
*	*				*			*		3–8	290	Sedum
*	*			*	*		*			4–9	294	Shasta Daisy
*				*	*		*			3–9	296	Sneezeweed
*					*			*		3–7	298	Soapwort
*	*			*	*			*		3–8	300	Speedwell
*	*			*			*			3–9	304	Spiderwort
*				*	*		*	*		4–9	306	Stokes' Aster
*					*			*	*	3–8	308	Sundrops
*					*	*		*	*	3–8	310	Thrift
*					*	*		*	*	4–8	312	Thyme
*	*			*	*		*	*		4–7	316	Trillium
	*	*	*	*	*		*	*	*	4–9	318	Vinca
	*	*	*	*		*	*	*		4–8	320	Wild Ginger
*					*	*		*	*	3–9	322	Yarrow

Glossary

Acid soil: soil with a pH below 7.0

Alkaline soil: soil with a pH above 7.0

Basal leaves: leaves that form from the crown

Crown: the part of a plant at or just below soil level where the shoots join the roots

Cultivar: a cultivated plant variety with one or more distinct differences from the species, e.g., in flower color, leaf variegation or disease resistance

Damping off: fungal disease causing seedlings to rot at soil level and topple over

Deadhead: to remove spent flowers to maintain a neat appearance and encourage a longer blooming period

Disbud: to remove some flowerbuds to improve the size or quality of the remaining ones

Dormancy: a period of plant inactivity, usually during winter or other unfavorable climatic conditions

Double flower: a flower with an unusually large number of petals, often caused by mutation of the stamens into petals

Genus: a category of biological classification between the species and family levels; the first word in a scientific name indicates the genus

Hardy: capable of surviving unfavorable conditions, such as cold weather

Humus: decomposed or decomposing organic material in the soil

Hybrid: a plant resulting from natural or human-induced crossbreeding between varieties, species or genera; the hybrid usually expresses features of each parent plant

Neutral soil: soil with a pH of 7.0

Node: the area on a stem from which a leaf or new shoot grows

Offset: a young plantlet that sprouts around the base of the parent plant

pH: a measure of acidity or alkalinity (the lower the pH, the higher the acidity); the pH of soil influences availability of nutrients for plants

Rhizome: a food-storing, root-like stem that grows horizontally at or just below soil level, from which new shoots may emerge

Rootball: the root mass and surrounding soil of a container-grown plant or a plant dug out of the ground

Semi-double flower: a flower with petals that form two or three rings

Semi-hardy: a plant capable of surviving the climatic conditions of a given region if protected

Single flower: a flower with a single ring of typically four or five petals

Species: the fundamental unit of biological classification; the original plant from which cultivars are derived

Subspecies (subsp.): a naturally occurring, regional form of a species, often isolated from other subspecies but still potentially interfertile with them

Taproot: a root system consisting of one main vertical root with smaller roots branching from it

Tender: incapable of surviving the climatic conditions of a given region; requiring protection from frost or cold

True: describes the passing of desirable characteristics from the parent plant to seed-grown offspring; also called breeding true to type

Tuber: the thick section of a rhizome bearing nodes and buds

Variegation: foliage that has more than one color, often patched or striped or bearing differently colored leaf margins

Variety (var.): a naturally occurring variant of a species; below the level of subspecies in biological classification

Index